Too
SOON
to
QUIT!

WARREN W. WIERSBE

TOO SOON to QUIT!

*Fifteen Achievers from the Bible Teach Us
How to Keep Going and How to Finish Well*

CLC
PUBLICATIONS
Fort Washington, PA 19034

Too Soon to Quit!

ISBN 10: 1-936143-00-3
ISBN 13 (trade paper): 978-1-936143-00-9
ISBN 13 (e-book): 978-1-936143-43-6

Copyright 2010 Warren W. Wiersbe

This edition 2012

Published by CLC Publications

U.S.A.
P.O. Box 1449, Fort Washington, PA 19034

GREAT BRITAIN
51 The Dean, Alresford, Hants. SO24 9BJ

Contents

Introduction

"It's always too soon to quit!"

The students at Wheaton College, Wheaton, Illinois frequently heard those words from Dr. V. Raymond Edman, former missionary to Ecuador, professor and, for twenty-five years, beloved president of the school. He spoke those words to the campus family in chapel as well as personally to individuals who were discouraged: "It's always too soon to quit."

Those six words are the theme of this book.

I began my ministry in the middle of the last century, when Harry Truman was president, Senator Joseph McCarthy was investigating the State Department and you could fly round trip from New York City to California for $88. I was still in seminary, and between class assignments I had four speaking ministries each week at the church I was serving. Along with funerals, weddings, committee meetings and various evangelical emergencies, I was one busy pastor, and there were days when I was tempted to quit. I almost got an ulcer during our church building program, but we kept on going. Our dear people put up with me, prayed, sacrificed and worked together and the Lord blessed.

This was followed by four years on the staff of Youth for Christ International. Each staff member had two or three jobs but only one salary, and we had to pray that salary in—but what years of blessing God gave us! I was traveling a good deal, and when not on the road I was working at the office and at home. The Lord would solve one problem and two others would appear, but we didn't quit. Ted Engstrom would close the office, the staff would go to a nearby church and spend hours in praise and prayer, and the Lord would bare His arm and meet our needs. Difficult as those four years were, my wife and I wouldn't take anything in exchange for the faith lessons that stretched our spiritual muscles.

Our next assignment was Calvary Baptist Church in Covington, Kentucky, across the Ohio River from Cincinnati, where we enjoyed ten wonderful years and launched another building program. Then the Lord sent us to Moody Church in Chicago. Our closing "official ministry" was at Back to the Bible in Lincoln, Nebraska, which has been our home since 1982. During these fifty plus years, I've also been writing, speaking at conferences and churches, teaching in doctor of ministry programs in different schools, and trying to be a good example, mentor and encourager to the younger generation. More than once my wife has reminded me, "It's always too soon to quit."

This book is about fifteen Bible characters who refused to quit. They were in different situations, they had different gifts and personalities, and they faced different challenges, yet they kept on going and finished the race triumphantly. In my personal Bible study, I've tried to get to know these people better and discover the principles behind their steadfastness and courage. In these chapters I've shared what God has taught me. I know I still have much more to learn, but the condition of the church today convinces me that we need Christian leaders who won't quit. Who knows? You may be the very one God is looking for (see Ezek. 22:30).

You and I can be both encouraged and warned by the people God has used in the past.

This is not "ancient history" because today's world isn't dramatically different from the world they lived in. The scenery and equipment may change from decade to decade, but the cast and the script remain pretty much the same, and the unchanging God still directs the production. As Stuart Hamblen expressed it, "What He's done for others, He can do for you."[1] Trust Him!

I may be wrong, but it seems that there is a desperate need today for more godly leadership in our churches, schools and parachurch ministries. We need Christian men and women who have devoted the time and effort to let God train and equip them for leading His people. Education is important, but beyond that they must possess spiritual experience in the trenches, maturity in the Word of God and prayer, and the ability to work effectively with God's people to help them achieve their best.

We need people who agree that it's always too soon to quit, which is the message of this book.

Warren W. Wiersbe

1

Abraham, the Outsider

Outlook determines outcome.

I have served on the boards and staffs of several evang-elical ministries, a privilege that involved the awesome responsibility of reviewing job applications and sometimes interviewing applicants. As a pastor I have selected staff members and helped to enlist church officers. Let me admit that these tasks were not easy and that I made my share of mistakes. Looks can deceive you and so can résumés and letters of recommendation. (Some people's geese are all swans to them.) Men and women who, to me, didn't appear qualified turned out to be eminently successful in their work. Others who seemed destined to turn the world upside down ended up quietly bowing out, never to be heard from again. I've had to remind myself often of what the Lord says in Isaiah 55:8–9:

> "For my thoughts are not your thoughts, neither are your ways my ways," declares the LORD. "As the heavens are higher than the earth, so are my ways higher than your ways and my thoughts than your thoughts."

Or, as Dr. Bob Cook used to tell us in Youth for Christ, "If you can explain what's going on, God didn't do it."

Abraham and Sarah: An Unexpected Choice

Suppose you and I had been consulted about how the Lord should expedite His great plan of salvation to save a lost world. *Would we have started by choosing Abraham and Sarah?* Probably not, and let me explain why.

To begin with, society today is obsessed with numbers, and for God to choose just two people seems a dangerous gamble. From our viewpoint God would have been wiser to use the big crowd that built the tower of Babel. Until the Lord put the whole enterprise out of business, they had accomplished something to be *proud* of! (And pride was the very thing that was wrong with it!) "Big is beautiful" may be a clever slogan, but God still asks, "Who dares despise the day of small things?" (Zech. 4:10). Jacob and his family went down to Egypt and eventually became a great nation. A few loaves and fishes fed thousands. Little is much if God is in it. God said of Abraham, "When I called him he was only one man, and I blessed him and made him many" (Isa. 51:2). The key isn't numbers but the miracle power of God.

Society is also obsessed with youth, but Abraham and Sarah were old. She was sixty-five and he was seventy-five, too old to have a family. But Jehovah is "the God who gives life to the dead and calls into being things that were not" (Rom. 4:17). When God wanted to kill a blaspheming giant, He put a sling and five stones into the hands of David, a shepherd boy, and David killed Goliath. When God wanted to destroy an invading army that looked like a swarm of locusts, He drafted a frightened farmer named Gideon and gave him three hundred men whose only weapons were pitchers and torches, and they wiped out the enemy. Our God is the God of the impossible.

Another thing people today focus on is speed—automobiles, airplanes, rockets, e-mail—yet God waited twenty-five years before giving Abraham and Sarah their son Isaac. And then Isaac had to grow up and find a wife, and he was forty years old before he married. But that isn't all: the Lord waited twenty more years after Isaac and Rebekah were married before He gave them children, Jacob and Esau. God took eighty-five years to get around to the birth of Jacob, the father of the twelve sons who founded the twelve tribes of Israel; and, of course, Jacob had to grow up before he could get married and start a family. It was centuries before Mary was born and given the privilege of bringing the Son of God into the world. It doesn't appear that God is in a hurry, but we must remember that His ways are not our ways. Our times are in His hands (Ps. 31:15).

The modern world is also fascinated by innovation but scornful of tradition. Like the Athenians in Paul's day, many people do nothing but get involved in the latest fads (Acts 17:21). People stand in line to purchase the latest gimmicks, and no sooner do they learn how to use them than the manufacturers declare the models obsolete. Innovation! Progress! But in accomplishing the great work of redemption, God used very traditional methods: men and women fell in love, got married and had children, as the Bible genealogies make clear. Very traditional. It was only when Jesus was conceived by the Holy Spirit in Mary's womb that God broke with tradition and performed a miracle.

Finally, our world is caught up in celebrity worship. The American humorist Fred Allen defined a celebrity as "a person who works hard . . . to become well known, then wears dark glasses to avoid being recognized." Many newspapers have a "celebrity" column so we can follow their tracks daily; slick magazines and garish tabloids are devoted to exposing their hidden secrets; and the television and movie industries would probably collapse without them. *But Abraham and Sarah were not celebrities!* They were common folk who trusted God and followed His call, and He used them to found the nation of Israel. Yes, God can use celebrities, but His usual approach is to call "the foolish things of this world to shame the wise . . . the weak things of the world to shame the strong . . . the lowly things of this world and the despised things . . . to nullify the things that are, so that no one may boast before him" (see 1 Cor. 1:26–31).

Let's agree that the Lord did the right thing when He called Abraham and Sarah. And when you and I have ministry decisions to make, let's imitate Abraham and Sarah and not the crowd at the tower of Babel. And let's not forget that their most important responsibility was to obey God and remain outsiders, separated from the godlessness around them but not isolated from the people they needed to reach with the truth.

Called Out of Paganism

When God's call came, they were citizens of Ur of the Chaldeans, "a great city and . . . a highly organized civilization," according to the eminent archaeologist Sir Leonard Wooley. Ur had a population of over 300,000 and was surrounded by lush land that produced wheat and barley, and supported orchards that bore dates and figs. Located on the Euphrates River, the city was involved in profitable trade and commerce. Most of the people lived in comfort and some of them in luxury, for archaeologists have unearthed fourteen-room villas. The city was dedicated to the moon god Nanna and his consort and contained large temples to their honor. Abraham and Sarah worshiped idols (Josh. 24:1–3).

"The God of glory appeared to our father Abraham," Stephen tells us, and the God of the Word spoke to him (Acts 7:1–3). Once Abraham saw God's glory, the pagan gods became ugly, and when Abraham heard the Lord speak to him, the mute idols became worthless. The Lord said, "Go from your country, your people and your father's household to the land I will show you" (Gen. 12:1). This dramatic experience transformed Abraham, and when he shared the news with Sarah, she also believed and with her husband turned her back on Ur, the city to which Abraham would never want to return (Gen. 24:1–9). Abraham didn't know where they were going on earth (Heb. 11:8), but he knew what the future held for them in heaven. "For he was looking forward to the city with foundations, whose architect and builder is God" (Heb. 11:10).

That first step of faith in the true and living God had changed their citizenship. They were now "foreigners and strangers on earth" (Heb. 11:13). Abraham was an outsider. A vagabond has no home, a fugitive is running from home, a stranger is away from home, but a pilgrim is heading home. Outlook determines outcome, and their outlook was really an upward look. It was this upward look that kept them going when circumstances upset them and God seemed to have forgotten them.

The most important thing about Abraham and Sarah is that they became outsiders, and as long as they remained outsiders, they enjoyed God's blessing. Whenever they ran ahead of God and did their own thing, or tried to run away from one of God's faith-building tests, God had to discipline them and get them back on the right road. God's work is not accomplished by the compromising insiders or by the isolated outsiders. It's done by the separated outsiders who know how to walk with God in this world and have contact with sinners without participating in their sins. Abraham and Sarah were separated outsiders who brought blessing to the whole world. Lot became a compromising insider and lost everything.

Called to Obedience

"Go from your country, your people and your father's household to the land I will show you" (Gen. 12:1) was God's command to Abraham, words easy to understand. But Abraham made two serious mistakes as he began his faith journey: he took with him his father Terah and his nephew Lot, and when the party arrived at Haran, Abraham stopped being a traveler and became a settler

(Gen. 11:22–32). It wasn't until his father died that Abraham resumed the pilgrim journey. Abraham learned early that obedience to God's Word is the first evidence of true faith in God, and that disobedience can be costly. God wants us to end well, and Abraham did.

In Genesis 14:13, Abraham is called "the Hebrew," a word that comes from "Eber," the name of one of Abraham's ancestors (Gen. 10:24–25; 11:15). The word means "a region across or beyond." To the Gentile residents of Canaan, the "Hebrews" were unimportant outsiders, people who came from beyond and crossed the Euphrates River to enter Canaan. The Septuagint translates Genesais 14:13 "Abraham, the one who crossed over." You will find in Scripture the word "Hebrew" used in an insulting way by the Gentiles. Potiphar's wife called Joseph "that Hebrew slave" (Gen. 39:17), and the Philistine soldiers shouted at Jonathan and his armorbearer, "Look! . . . The Hebrews are crawling out of the holes they were hiding in" (1 Sam. 14:11). As far as the residents of Canaan were concerned, the Hebrews were outsiders, guests in the land, people without citizenship and without value.

But it didn't really matter what the neighbors called Abraham because he had another title that nobody else could claim: he was "the friend of God" (2 Chron. 20:7; Isa. 41:8; James 2:23). That's why his tent and altar were important, for they marked him as a man separated from the other people in the land. Abraham was a man of faith; his eyes were on the heavenly city and not on the cities of the plain such as Sodom. Lot finally settled in Sodom because Lot was a friend of the world (James 4:4–6). Read John 15:9–17 and you will discover that Jesus has called His disciples "friends." What privileges we have! Why turn to the world for help?

Called to Be a Pilgrim

After burying his father, Abraham led the party south and they stopped at Shechem (Gen. 12:6), a lovely area in a green valley with orchards, gardens and springs, not unlike the land around Ur. Then he moved between Bethel ("house of God") and Ai ("heap of ruins") and set up his camp. Can you see in Abraham and Sarah a picture of Christian believers today? We are pilgrims who are supposed to make progress, and we are living between this world ("a heap of ruins") and the eternal house of God in heaven (John 14:1–6).

Abraham gave a powerful personal witness to the people around him simply by the way he lived, and so should we. He admitted he was an outsider (Gen. 23:4) and they knew he lived in a tent. His home was temporary and he was ready to move whenever God gave the order. He built an altar and worshiped, not a god of wood, metal or stone, but the true and living God in heaven. He was wealthy enough to build himself a fine house, but pilgrims don't live in houses; they live in tents. Paul called the Christian's body "the earthly tent we live in" (2 Cor. 5:1–5). More about this later.

But then something unexpected happened: there was a famine in the land to which God had called Abraham (Gen. 12:10–20). Abraham and Sarah already had their share of trials and they probably expected Canaan to be their safe haven, but it was not. They had buried Abraham's brother back in Ur and had made the long journey from

Ur to Haran where they buried Abraham's father. You can bury the dead and you can survive a difficult journey, but how do you handle a famine? If we are walking by faith, we commit ourselves to the Lord and wait for His next assignment, trusting Him to provide what we need. But Abraham panicked and began to walk by sight and fled to Egypt.

In the "spiritual geography" of the Bible, Egypt stands for "the world," which means society without God, the whole system of people, things, ideas, priorities and goals that are contrary to the will of God but that run the anti-God system today. "For everything in the world—the cravings of sinful people, the lust of their eyes and their boasting about what they have and do—comes not from the Father but from the world. The world and its desires pass away, but whoever does the will of God lives forever" (1 John 2:16–17). Jesus called Satan "the prince of this world" (John 12:31) because he has certain powers and privileges that enable him to use the world and the things in the world to entice God's people and oppose God's work (Matt. 4:8–10).

Whenever we find ourselves in difficult circumstances, we can trust God, wait and grow, or we can turn the situation into a temptation, refuse to believe God and end up disobeying Him. Abraham chose Plan B, fled to Egypt, lied about his wife and almost lost her. He ruined his testimony and left Egypt a very embarrassed man. As far as the record is concerned, Abraham abandoned his tent and altar while in Egypt; but when he returned to the Promised Land, he renewed his walk with the Lord (Gen. 13:1–4).

Outsiders do sin and make mistakes, but they admit their sins and go back where they belong, and God forgives them. The Scottish preacher George H. Morrison said, "The victorious Christian life is a series of new beginnings." You don't get saved over and over again, but you renew your walk with God and keep going. Outsiders can become backsliders, but they won't stay that way very long. They get their eyes back on the heavenly city, confess their sins and seek God's forgiveness, and He restores them.

Many individual believers and entire congregations have imitated Abraham and "run to Egypt" to get help. They stop being outsiders; they lose their separation from the world and start promoting imitation of the world. Sanctuaries become theaters, worship leaders become entertainers and everybody is happy except the Lord. The Word of God and prayer are minimized, booming music is maximized and the gospel is merchandised. This may be one way to build a crowd, but is it God's way to glorify Jesus Christ and build a church? Consider what Paul wrote in First Thessalonians 2:1–7 and take it to heart.

Learning to Obey—the Hard Way

When you read Abraham's life, you discover that, while he consistently moved in the right direction, occasionally he stumbled. After ten years on the faith trail, Abraham and Sarah were still childless, so Sarah suggested that her husband marry her maid Hagar and have a child by her (Gen. 16). This kind of marriage was perfectly legal in that day, but many things that are legal are not necessarily the will of God. *What Abraham brought with him out of Egypt only got him into trouble!* The wealth he acquired ("atonement money" from Pharaoh) would create problems between him and Lot (Gen. 13), and Hagar would bring Ishmael—Abraham's firstborn son—into the world and threaten the home. The day came when Hagar and Ishmael had to go (Gen. 21:8–10). Imagine how painful this experience must have been for Abraham!

Abraham went down to Gerar and again lied about his wife (Gen. 20). The Lord dealt with Abimelek, king of Gerar, and exposed Abraham's deception and the "family secret" Sarah and Abraham carried since leaving Ur. The king soundly rebuked Abraham, then generously gave him "atonement money" and sent him on his way. Again, Abraham and Sarah made a fresh beginning, and God kept His promise and gave them a son (Gen. 21).

Then God asked Abraham to give that son back to Him! (See Genesis 22.) This was his ultimate test in the school of faith, for the future of God's gracious plan of salvation rested with that son. Without Isaac there would be no Jacob, and without Jacob there would be no twelve tribes of Israel. Without the nation of Israel there would be no witness of the true and living God, no holy Scripture and no Redeemer. Abraham had progressed in the school of faith and passed this test to the glory of God.

God is sovereign, and when He isn't allowed to rule, He overrules. We occasionally stumble, but that isn't the end of the story. "The LORD makes firm the steps of those who delight in him; though they stumble, they will not fall, for the Lord holds them by the hand" (Ps. 37:23–24 NLT).

Outlook determines outcome, and Abraham's outlook was really up-look, because "he was looking forward to the city with foundations, whose architect and builder is God" (Heb. 11:10). This is the equivalent of Hebrews 12:2, "fixing our eyes on Jesus, the pioneer and perfecter of our faith." Paul put it this way: "But one thing I do: Forgetting what is behind and straining toward what is ahead, I press on toward the goal to win the prize for which God has called me heavenward in Christ Jesus" (Phil. 3:13–14).

Called to Be Different

Like their forefather Abraham, the people of Israel were supposed to be outsiders, separated from the evil of the world. "I am the LORD your God who has set you apart from the nations.... You are to be holy to me because I, the LORD, am holy, and I have set you apart from the nations to be my own" (Lev. 20:24, 26). The seer Balaam said, "I see a people who live apart and do not consider themselves one of the nations" (Num. 23:9). When Solomon dedicated the temple, he mentioned the uniqueness of Israel: "For you singled them out from all the nations of the world to be your own inheritance" (1 Kings 8:53). Wicked Haman told King Xerxes, "There is a certain people dispersed among the peoples in all the provinces of your kingdom who keep themselves separate" (Esther 3:8). In Romans 9:4–5 Paul names some of the privileges God gave to Israel that He gave to no other nation.

> Theirs is the adoption; theirs the divine glory, the covenants, the receiving of the law, the temple worship and the promises. Theirs are the patriarchs, and from them is traced the human ancestry of the Messiah, who is God over all, forever praised! Amen.

This is why the Lord commanded the Jewish people to have nothing to do with the people and practices of the nations in Canaan. "Break down their altars, smash their sacred stones and cut down their Asherah poles" (Exod. 34:13; see Deut. 7). They were not to intermarry with them or make covenants with them. They were not even to salvage the precious metals and jewels they would see in the pagan idols they destroy (Deut. 7:25–26).

Even before Israel crossed the Jordan River and entered the Promised Land, they fraternized with the enemy (Num. 25). The Moabites invited the Jews to share one of their feasts, and the Jews disobeyed God and attended. But the feast was devoted to idolatry and immorality, and God had to judge His people and kill over 24,000 disobedient Israelites.

No sooner had the Jews fought their first battle in the Promised Land than Achan, one of the soldiers, coveted some of the spoils from Jericho and brought defeat to the army of Israel at Ai and death to himself and his family (Josh. 7). The Israelites maintained their separation during the leadership of Joshua and the elders who succeeded him; but when the third generation took over the leadership, they forsook the Lord and His law, and followed the ways of the pagan nations around them (see Judg. 2:6–23). They worshiped the gods of the defeated enemy!

The Book of Judges records a cycle of repeated unfaithfulness on the part of the people of Israel. As long as a godly judge was in charge, the people obeyed God at least outwardly; but when the judge died, the people descended again into idolatry. Then God brought a Gentile nation to chastise and enslave the Israelites in their own land. The Israelites would cry out to God for mercy, and in His grace He would deliver them and give them a new leader; but the cycle would be repeated six times! Frequently during the period of the divided kingdom, during the years the prophets ministered, Israel imitated Abraham and went down to Egypt for help (Isa. 30:1–5; Jer. 2:12–19; 42–43). Both the northern and southern kingdoms resorted to idolatrous practices, and God finally brought Assyria to destroy the northern kingdom of Israel and Babylon to take the southern kingdom of Judah into captivity.

After the Babylonian captivity, when only a remnant of Jews returned to Jerusalem to rebuild the city and the temple, one of their major problems was keeping the Israelites separated from the pagan Gentiles (Ezra. 6:21; 9–10; Neh. 9–10; 13:23–31). Israel was meant to be a light to the Gentiles (Isa. 42:6; 49:6), but instead, the Gentiles put heavy burdens on the Jews! By the time we get to the end of the Old Testament, only a remnant of the Jewish people are faithful to the Lord and watching for the arrival of the promised Redeemer (Mal. 3:16–18). We meet some of them in the first two chapters of Luke: Zechariah and Elizabeth, Mary and Joseph, the Judean shepherds, and Simeon and Anna.

Social Outsiders, Spiritual Insiders

Abraham was an outsider and his natural descendants —the nation of Israel—were supposed to live like outsiders, but they failed. They repeatedly sinned against their privileged position and invited the discipline of the Lord. But Abraham also has *spiritual* descendants, those who have put their faith in Jesus Christ and been born into God's family. "Understand, then, that those who have faith are children of Abraham. . . . So those who rely on faith are blessed along with Abraham, the man of faith. . . . If you belong to Christ, then you are Abraham's seed, and heirs according to the promise" (Gal. 3:7, 9, 29).

The church, then, is a fellowship of outsiders, living in a hostile world. When Jesus prayed for His church, He said, "My prayer is not that you take them out of the world but that you protect them from the evil one. They are not of the world, even as I am not of it" (John 17:15–16). He has overcome the world system (John 16:33) and left us in this world of humanity to bear witness through word and deed of the good news of redemption. The world sees Christians as outsiders, but from God's point of view, *it's the unsaved who are the outsiders*. "Be wise in the way you act toward outsiders; make the most of every opportunity" (Col. 4:5). "You should mind your own business and work with your hands . . . so that your daily life may win the respect of outsiders" (1 Thess. 4:11–12). Church leaders "must have a good reputation with outsiders" (1 Tim. 3:7). Believers are in the world but not of the world, while the unsaved are in the world, of the world and outside the family of God. The world is the sea out of which we seek to "catch" as many as we can with the gospel net (Matt. 13:47–50).

But history shows that God's people frequently imitated the world and acted like the outsiders they were trying to evangelize. Paul admonished the believers in Rome, "Do not be conformed to the pattern of this world, but be transformed by the renewing of your mind" (Rom.

12:2). Christians are not supposed to be odd, but they are supposed to be different. The believers in Corinth were living like unbelievers, and Paul wrote to them, "Therefore, if anyone is in Christ, the new creation has come: the old has gone, the new is here!" (2 Cor. 5:17). Peter had a similar message for the believers in the Roman provinces: "As obedient children, do not conform to the evil desires you had when you lived in ignorance. But just as he who called you is holy, so be holy in all you do; for it is written, 'Be holy, because I am holy'" (1 Pet. 1:14–16).

When the church starts imitating the world, it ceases to incarnate the Lord and glorify Him. If God is truly at work in and through us, then we will magnify Jesus Christ before "a warped and crooked generation" and "shine like stars in the sky" (see Phil. 2:12–16). "Whatever happens, as citizens of heaven live in a manner worthy of the gospel of Christ" (Phil. 1:27; see also 3:17–20). Those outside the family of God don't understand the Word of the Lord, and it's our responsibility to use every legitimate means possible to teach them (Mark 4:11).

Abraham's life was identified with a tent and an altar. He was a pilgrim, an alien in transit, and he was a worshiper of the one true and living God. How do individual believers and churches today bear the same kind of witness? Are we pilgrims—or settlers?

Aliens in a Foreign Land

"Some Christians are so heavenly minded, they are no earthly good." Evangelist D. L. Moody used to make that statement, and it needs to be heard today. If we are confident that we are going to heaven, our assurance should make a difference in our daily lives.

Abraham kept his eyes of faith on his heavenly home, but he didn't ignore what was happening in the neighborhood. When the land was at war, he armed his men and with God's help defeated the enemy—and took nothing for his services (Gen. 14). When he learned that the Lord was about to destroy Sodom and Gomorrah, Abraham interceded for the city, thinking especially of Lot and his family (Gen. 18). When he had the sad responsibility of burying his wife Sarah, he paid more than a fair price for the cave of Machpelah (Gen. 23). He made certain that his son Isaac married a woman from within the family so that the covenant with the Lord could be fulfilled. He let his light shine and the residents knew he was different.

When the people of the northern kingdom were in exile in Babylon, the prophet Jeremiah sent them a letter instructing them how to live as aliens in a foreign land (Jer. 29). He didn't advise them to organize demonstrations, form an underground movement or protest against the government. Among other things, this is what the Lord commanded them to do:

> Build houses and settle down; plant gardens and eat what they produce. Marry and have sons and daughters; find wives for your sons and give your daughters in marriage, so that they too may have sons and daughters. Increase in number there; do not decrease. Also, seek the peace and prosperity of the city to which I have carried you into exile. Pray to the Lord for it, because if it prospers, you too will prosper. (Jer. 29:5–7)

In short, God told them to live normal godly lives and be a part of the answer, not part of the problem.

After you read Jeremiah's letter, read Peter's first epistle and note how they agree. Peter wrote "to God's elect, exiles [strangers] scattered throughout" the Roman provinces (1 Pet. 1:1). Jeremiah's exiles were in Babylon. In 1:17 Peter exhorted the believers to "live out [their] time as foreigners here in reverent fear," and in 2:11 he called them "foreigners and exiles." Peter's letter to the Christians resembles Jeremiah's letter to the exiles in Babylon, and both letters have wise counsel for the church of Jesus Christ today.

"Submit yourselves for the Lord's sake to every human authority," Peter wrote, "whether to the emperor, as the supreme authority, or to governors who are sent by him to punish those who do wrong and to commend those who do right. For it is God's will that by doing good you should silence the ignorant talk of the foolish. . . . Show proper respect to everyone, love your fellow believers, fear God, honor the emperor" (1 Pet. 2:13–15, 17). But note that Peter not only emphasizes a right attitude toward pagan authority but also a loving relationship within the church family. *The loving unity of God's people is a tremendous witness in this shattered world.* (See especially 1 Peter 3:8–4:19.)

The word "called" is a key word in Peter's first letter and helps us understand the responsibilities we have as pilgrims and strangers.

- We are called to be holy in this evil world (1:15–16).
- We are called to shine as lights in a dark world (2:9).

- We are called to follow the example of Christ because the world opposes and persecutes us as it did Him (2:21).
- We are called to inherit a blessing as we return good for evil (3:9–12).
- We are called to enter God's glory, come what may (5:8–11).

Meditate on those verses and see how they are illustrated in the life of Abraham.

It has often been pointed out that many churches are not lights revealing the godlessness of today's culture and the glory of the Lord, but mirrors reflecting the culture. Instead of worship leaders, we have cheerleaders presiding over pep rallies. Few people miss the spiritual power of Acts 1:8 because the churches are amply supplied with technology; and as for the proclamation of good news for sinners, the church offers only good advice and good feelings Why? Because God's people feel very much at home in this "present evil age" (Gal. 1:4) and would rather be comfortable in the world than conformed to the Savior. Like Lot, we are settlers, not strangers and pilgrims. We are no longer outsiders. We have so adjusted to the world that we are one with those who are outside God's family, but at great cost.

Called to Be the Church

Back in the sixties one of the popular slogans of many so-called "street Christians" was "Jesus, yes! The church, no!" Media people had a good time with this shibboleth because it provided opportunities to criticize the church and those of us who are a part of it. But how can anybody who claims to be a member of God's family love the Bridegroom and despise His Bride? How can they give honor to the Head and ignore His Body?

Certainly we who are a part of the church confess our faults and failures and weep over them; but we're staying with the church and doing our best to help it live up to its heavenly calling. Like Abraham, we are not going to quit. We will keep looking up, focusing our attention on heaven and the promised return of our Lord Jesus Christ.

Outlook Determines Outcome

It worked for Abraham and it will work for us: "fixing our eyes on Jesus, the pioneer and perfecter of faith. . . . Therefore, since we are receiving a kingdom that cannot be shaken, let us be thankful, and so worship God acceptably with reverence and awe, for our God is a consuming fire" (Heb. 12:2, 28–29).

2

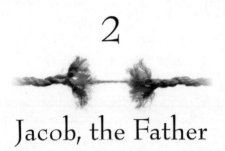

Jacob, the Father

God never stops loving His children.

What do you do in the course of your Bible reading when you come to a genealogy? Be honest, now!

Do you scan the names and then go on to read the narrative, or do you ignore the genealogy completely? After all, what kind of spiritual nutrition can you find in a list of names difficult to pronounce and boring to read? It's like reading a telephone directory!

Jacob is, in a way, the man responsible for those ancient historical documents; they record the names of his descendants. He was the grandson of Abraham, the son of Isaac, the brother of Esau and the father of the twelve men who founded the twelve tribes of Israel. Genesis 25:21–26 informs us that Jacob and his twin brother Esau were answers to prayer, for Isaac and Rebekah had been married twenty years before the boys arrived. At least one-fourth of the book of Genesis is devoted to Jacob's history, so he is a significant man.

The ancient Jews respected and protected their genealogies. These records were the official "family tree" that identified their tribes and families, defined who they could marry and who could inherit property. When the Jews returned to their land after the Babylonian captivity, the genealogies were the only means they had for identifying those who were truly Jews, priests and Levites, and where these people could live.

Even more importantly, those ancient names are living links in God's plan of salvation that culminated in the birth of Jesus Christ, the Son of God and the Savior of the world. The last genealogies in the Bible are those of Jesus Christ (Matt. 1; Luke 3:23–37), and they prove that, in His humanity, He is from the tribe of Judah, of the family of David and is the legitimate heir to David's throne. "Salvation is from the Jews," said our Lord (John 4:22). While Abraham and Isaac got things started, it was Jacob whom God used to build the Jewish nation. Remember this the next time you breeze through a genealogy as though reading it were a waste of time.

A "Dysfunctional" Family

Jacob's life wasn't easy.

He didn't have an easy life at home. He and his twin brother Esau were opposites. Jacob was a quiet homebody and enjoyed being in his tent, while Esau was an adventurous outdoorsman who spent days hunting game in the fields and forests. The home was divided: Isaac favored Esau (and the venison he cooked) and Rebekah favored Jacob. Both Isaac and Rebekah knew that God had ordained Jacob to receive the family blessing and birthright (Gen. 25:23), but Isaac chose to ignore God's will (Gen. 27:1–4), while Rebekah chose to accomplish

God's will her own way. Years before, they had prayed for sons and God had answered, but now praying was replaced by scheming. Jacob conned his brother out of the birthright (Gen. 25:27–34), and Jacob and his mother teamed up to obtain the blessing of the firstborn for Jacob. They didn't wait for God to act in His time.

Acting like the man of the world he was, Esau threatened to kill his brother, so Rebekah sent Jacob 500 miles away to the home of her brother Laban in Paddan Aram. "Stay with him for a while," she said, but that "while" lasted for two decades, and Rebekah never saw her favorite son again. This change in geography, however, didn't solve Jacob's problems; if anything, it made them worse. Jacob's Uncle Laban was a liar and a thief and made Jacob's life miserable for the next twenty years.

But Jacob met the Lord at Bethel (Gen. 28:10–22), and for the future father of the people of Israel, that meeting would mean the difference between success and failure.

Family Deception, Family Conflict

No sooner did he arrive in Paddan Aram than Jacob fell in love with Laban's younger daughter Rachel. Laban approved their marriage provided Jacob shepherded his flocks for seven years. Jacob joyfully fulfilled the agreement, but Laban gave him Leah instead of Rachel, explaining that local custom required the elder daughter to marry first. Why didn't Laban tell him that seven years before? Probably because it wasn't true. After the week of wedding celebration, Laban gave him Rachel and asked for another seven years of work. That's fourteen years' work for two wives, and Jacob wanted only Rachel. The deceiver had been deceived.

But the plot thickens. Leah was more fertile than Rachel and gave Jacob four sons, one after the other, and later two more sons and a daughter. "Give me children, or I'll die!" cried Rachel (Gen. 30:1), blaming Jacob for her barrenness, and Jacob responded by blaming God. (This defense has its origin in Genesis 3:8–13.) Rachel's solution was to have Jacob marry her handmaid Bilhah, who bore him two sons. Leah liked this plan, so her maid Zilpah became Jacob's fourth wife, and she also bore him two sons. Rachel had been praying for a child, and God answered and gave her Joseph (Gen. 30:22–24). Envy, rivalry, competition and unbelief marked the personal dynamics of the family. When Jacob came home from the fields, he never knew which wife he would be sleeping with, and one night Leah even "rented" Jacob from Rachel (Gen. 30:14–16)!

If Jacob was home, he had problems, and if he was in the fields, he had worse problems, for Laban was a crafty taskmaster. After working fourteen years for Leah and Rachel, Jacob wanted to return to his parental home, but Laban was loath to let him go. He didn't want to lose the blessing of the Lord that Jacob had brought with him.

However, this time Jacob was ahead of Laban. He offered to care for Laban's flocks without wages if he could begin to build his own flocks from the spotted and speckled animals among Laban's sheep and goats. These were considered inferior animals, so Laban happily agreed. Jacob moved his flocks a three days' journey away from his father-in-law's flocks, and God increased and strengthened Jacob's flocks so that he became a very wealthy man. But Laban repeatedly blamed him for the animals of his flocks that were lost or died, and he made Jacob reimburse him! To keep the books balanced, he changed Jacob's wages ten times!

After seven years, the Lord told Jacob to go back home. Instead of being honorable and leaving openly, he attempted to leave by stealth, but Laban caught up with him. Had the Lord not warned Laban in a dream not to mistreat Jacob, their encounter might have become a catastrophe; but Jacob stood his ground and Laban backed down. They didn't really solve their differences but they did come to a truce and promise not to enter each other's territory because the Lord was watching them.

Jacob had his share of trouble as he made his way home. His past caught up with him when he met Esau, and the Lord had to wrestle with Jacob and cripple him to get him to trust instead of bargain. At Shechem his daughter Dinah was raped, and his sons Simeon and Levi became murderers. After pausing at Bethel for a family dedication service, they moved on to Bethlehem where Jacob's favorite wife Rachel died after giving birth to Benjamin. At Hebron Jacob reunited with his father, and then Isaac died. Yet there was still no peace at home, for the brothers were jealous of Joseph—this was partly Jacob's fault for pampering him—and sold him for a slave. They told their father Joseph was dead, and Jacob never ceased to mourn for his son. "Everything is against me!" cried Jacob (Gen. 42:36), when actually God was working everything *for* him that the family might be preserved and build the nation.

It was a time of intense grief for the old father until he learned that Joseph was alive and had prepared a home in Egypt for his family. Jacob was 130 years old when he traveled to Egypt with his family and saw Joseph again. There he enjoyed seventeen years of peace before he died and was taken back to Canaan for burial in the family tomb.

Jacob's Secret Strength

So much for the facts of history. Now let's consider the truths behind those facts and discover what it was that kept Jacob going when everything and everybody seemed to be working against him.

I believe that the secret of Jacob's overcoming power is this: *he knew that, come what may, the Lord loved him.* Twice in the Bible we find God saying, "Jacob I have loved" (Mal. 1:2; Rom. 9:13), and from the time he met the Lord at Bethel (Gen. 28:10–22) until his move to Egypt (Gen. 46:1–4), the Lord gave him many evidences of His love. These evidences can encourage God's people today and keep us from giving up when things are tough.

The first evidence is obvious: because God loved Jacob, *He chose him.* Yes, Esau was the firstborn, but the Lord didn't choose him; instead, He chose Jacob, the second born. Before the boys were born, God had made this clear to Isaac and Rebekah (Gen. 25:21–23), and it wasn't a new thing, for the pattern had already been set. God chose Abel but not Cain, and Isaac but not Ishmael. Later, Jacob himself would choose Ephraim, Joseph's second born, and bypass Manasseh the firstborn son (Gen. 48). God rejects our first birth and in His grace offers us a second birth, a new birth from heaven. "Flesh gives birth to flesh," said Jesus, "but the Spirit gives birth to spirit" (see John 3:1–8).

God's electing grace isn't based on our character or our conduct, for the Lord had chosen Jacob before the twins had been born or had done anything either good or bad (Rom. 9:10–16). Paul wrote to the believers in Corinth,

> Brothers and sisters, think of what you were when you were called. Not many of you were wise by human standards; not many were influential; not many were of noble birth. But God chose the foolish things of the world to shame the wise; God chose the weak things of the world to shame the strong. God chose the lowly things of this world and the despised things—and the things that are not—to nullify the things that are, so that no one may boast before him. (1 Cor. 1:26–29)

People who think they deserve to be saved are only proving that they know nothing about themselves or God's grace, for salvation is "the gift of God—not by works, so that no one can boast" (Eph. 2:8).

It was revealed to Jacob at Bethel that he was God's chosen vessel to receive and pass on the covenant blessings that were first given to Abraham and then to Isaac. He was chosen, not because he was a good man, but because of God's love and electing grace. We call upon the Lord and He saves us (Acts 2:21; Rom. 10:10–13), and then we discover that we were first chosen by Him (Eph. 1:3–6).

Hearing God's Voice

This brings us to a second evidence of God's love: *He speaks to us.*

The vision Jacob had that night at Bethel taught him much about the Lord. He reigns in glory in heaven, His army of angels cares for us, and heaven is a home, for it had a staircase. Best of all, the Lord of heaven is our Father and cares for us. Bethel was indeed an awesome place, the very gate of heaven, the very house of God. He thought God was far away and angry with him, but he learned that He was right there with him and ready to help him! John 1:43–51 tells us that Jesus is our "staircase" to heaven, and through Him we have access to the Father.

What Jacob *saw* prepared him for what he *heard*, for it was what Jacob heard that gave him the courage and strength he needed for the journey that lay before him. He probably expected to hear the Lord scold him for the way he had acted at home, but God said nothing about his sins. Instead, the Lord reaffirmed the same covenant He had made with his father and grandfather. He also promised to be with him in his travels, provide for him, watch over him and bring him back to Bethel. Years later, God would communicate with Jacob about breeding his sheep and goats and about leaving Paddan Aram and returning home (Gen. 31:10–13). When Jacob moved to Egypt, God spoke loving words of assurance to him (Gen. 46:1–4).

If we want to have overcoming power, it's essential that we hear God's voice as we read and meditate on the Word of God. People irritate us and circumstances baffle us, but there is always a word from the Lord that quiets our hearts and encourages us to keep going. When we open the Bible, God opens His mouth, and if we are disciplined in waiting on Him daily, He always has exactly the promise, warning, admonition or assurance that we need.

Learning from Discipline

A third evidence that God loves us is that *He disciplines us.* Hebrews 12:1–13 focuses on Christians as athletes, running the race God planned for them and not giving up. Athletes must be disciplined if they expect to endure the challenge of the games and achieve a winning record. The word "discipline" is a close relative of the word "disciple," for Christ's disciples must obey the rules and submit to the training of their coach.

The fact that God disciplines us is proof that we are truly His children, for no father has the right to discipline somebody else's children. Satan is very subtle. When he tempts us, he says, "You can get away with this. It will help you." After we've sinned, he says, "You will never get away with this! You aren't even a child of God!" But then the Father lovingly chastens us, and in doing that, assures us that we are His children, "because the Lord disciplines those he loves and chastens everyone he accepts as his child" (Heb. 12:6; Prov. 3:11–12).

One of God's disciplines is to allow us to reap what we have sown. Jacob lied once to his father and his father-in-law repeatedly lied to him. Jacob stole the birthright from his brother, and Laban stole wages from Jacob. Jacob lied to his father about who he was, and Leah lied to Jacob about who she was. Jacob killed two goats so his mother could counterfeit one of Esau's famous dishes, and Jacob's sons killed a goat and put its blood on Joseph's garment so Jacob would believe his son had been killed by a beast.

We reap what we sow. God doesn't always intervene.

Charles Spurgeon said that God doesn't allow his children to sin successfully, and he was right. Abraham learned this when he fled to Egypt and lied about his wife, and Lot learned it when he moved into Sodom. Samson thought he could get away with sin but discovered he was wrong, and David made the same mistake.

Of course, we don't need ancient examples to convince us, do we? Each of us has experienced the discipline of God at one time or another. If not, we had better examine our hearts and see if we're truly born again.

Sometimes the Father gives us a *permanent* reminder to humble us and encourage us to be obedient. In Jacob's case it was the limp he received while wrestling with the Lord (Gen. 32:22–32). Paul had a thorn in the flesh that even his prayers could not remove (2 Cor. 12:1–10), but his weakness opened the way for the Lord to give him strength. It's remarkable how many well-known servants of God were physically handicapped, and yet they would tell you that the "handicap" was really a blessing in disguise.

His Purposes, in His Time

Here is a fourth evidence of God's faithful love: *He patiently fulfills His purposes in us and through us.*

God is not in a hurry. He kept Abraham and Sarah waiting twenty-five years before Isaac was born, and Isaac and Rebekah waited twenty years for Esau and Jacob. Jacob had to wait fourteen years to get the bride he really wanted, and then he had to serve six more years to build up his flocks so he could be independent, a total of twenty years. Twenty-two years passed between Joseph's betrayal by his brothers and the brothers' reconciliation in Egypt. God is not in a hurry because all His works are done in love. "Love is patient, love is kind" (1 Cor. 13:4). Let's be grateful that God takes His time.

Just before Jacob died, he "blessed" his sons and also revealed some of their secrets; and during his address, he cried out, "I look for your deliverance, Lord" (Gen. 49:18). The word translated "look" can also be translated "to wait patiently" (Ps. 40:1). All of his adult life, Jacob was learning to wait patiently, for impatience leads to impetuousness and both are marks of immaturity (James 1:2–7). He waited for the woman he loved. He waited for deliverance from Laban's galling yoke. He waited and wept after the report of Joseph's "death." He waited during his sons' trips to Egypt, praying that everybody was safe. He waited during the trip to Egypt.

But we must not forget that the greatest purpose of all in these matters was to bring the Son of God to this earth to give His life for the salvation of sinners. The word "deliverance" in Jacob's prayer is *yeshua*, and this is the first time it is found in the Bible. It means "salvation" and is the Hebrew word that gives us the name *Jesus*. When Mary's pregnancy worried her husband Joseph, an angel told him, "What is conceived in her is from the Holy Spirit. She will give birth to a son, and you are to give to him the name Jesus, because he will save his people from their sins" (Matt. 1:20–21).

"I wait for your *Yeshua*, Lord!" The nation of Israel would produce prophets and kings, priests and scholars, warriors and singers—and a Savior! Jesus was a gift worth waiting for.

God has a purpose for each of His children to fulfill (Eph. 2:10), and we must be patient as He works for us and within us to equip us to accomplish that purpose. When I was in seminary, I recall one of the discouraged students going to the registrar and announcing that he was dropping out of school. His argument was that the world was lost and he was wasting time studying when he could be out winning the lost.

The registrar listed patiently, complimented him on his burden for souls and then said: "The Lord has been waiting a long time for you to come along, and I'm sure He can wait one more year. Besides, being a good student and equipping yourself for service is just as much a ministry as preaching. God usually finishes what he starts; so if He brought you here, He probably wants you to stay and earn your degree." The student did stay in school and complete his work, and in the ensuing years, he was grateful that he did.

"Be still before the Lord and wait patiently for him" (Ps. 37:7).

"God acts on behalf of those who wait for Him" (Isa. 64:4).

"Being confident of this, that he who began a good work in you will carry it on to completion until the day of Jesus Christ" (Phil. 1:6).

Blessed to Be a Blessing

We know that God loves us because, in spite of our failures, *He makes us a blessing to others.*

One of my favorite scenes in Scripture is described in Genesis 47:7–10. Joseph is presenting his father to Pharaoh, and Pharaoh asks Jacob his age. Jacob replies, "The years of my pilgrimage are a hundred and thirty. My years have been few and difficult, and they do not equal the years of the pilgrimage of my fathers." The next sentence arrests me: "Then Jacob blessed Pharaoh . . ." Imagine! This aged Jewish shepherd is blessing the most powerful ruler in the ancient Near East in that day! And one reason why he could impart a blessing is because he had been a pilgrim on the move, not a comfortable settler, and had experienced many difficulties that brought to his own life the blessings of the Lord.

Jacob had been a blessing to his own family and to the family of his father-in-law Laban. He had certainly been a blessing to his sons. Jacob had enjoyed seventeen years with Joseph in Canaan, and now he would have seventeen more years with him in Egypt. The Lord had fulfilled His covenant promise, "I will bless you . . . and you will be a blessing" (Gen. 12:2–3). But most of all, Jacob has been a blessing to the whole world through the nation of Israel that gave us the Lord Jesus Christ. Yes, we can find fault with this man (and he with us!), but God Almighty is willing to call Himself "the God of Jacob." The Lord isn't ashamed to identify Himself with Jacob. "The Lord Almighty is with us; the God of Jacob is our fortress" (Ps. 46:7, 11).

What kept him going during those "few and difficult" years? *He knew that God loved him.* Like his believing father and grandfather, "he was looking forward to the city with foundations, whose architect and builder is

God" (Heb. 11:10). It is a city with a great, high wall and with twelve gates, and on the gates "were written the names of the twelve tribes of Israel" (Rev. 21:12)—the names of Jacob's sons!

> Who shall separate us from the love of Christ? Shall trouble or hardship or persecution or famine or nakedness or danger or sword? . . . No, in all these things we are more than conquerors through him who loved us. For I am convinced that neither death nor life, nor angels nor demons, neither the present nor the future, nor any powers, neither height nor depth, nor anything else in all creation, will be able to separate us from the love of God that is in Christ Jesus our Lord. (Rom. 8:35, 37–39)

We know that God's love never fails, so it's always too soon to quit.

3

Joseph, the Dreamer

Heaven's dreams surpass the world's delusions.

I read about a well-dressed man who was walking swiftly down a crowded metropolitan sidewalk and pausing frequently to chat with people along the way.

"I'm in trouble," the man would say. "I didn't dream last night, and I'm heading for my psychiatrist's office. All I'm trying to do is borrow a dream from somebody. Have you got one?"

Borrow a Dream?

Well, in *Joseph and the Amazing Technicolor Dreamcoat*, we're assured that "Any Dream Will Do," and in another musical we're told to "Dream the Impossible Dream." When the Mother Superior in *Sound of Music* sings to Maria, she advises her to climb mountains, ford streams and even follow rainbows until she "finds her dream." Each December, people start "dreaming of a white Christmas," and each January they commemorate the birthday of Martin Luther King, Jr. and remember his famous "I Have A Dream" speech.

The word "dream" has several meanings. A dream might be a series of mental images we "see" when we're asleep, or a dream might be a strange experience we have while we're awake. "It was so weird," we say, "as though I was dreaming!" Job's friend Zophar used the word dream as a simile to show the brevity of a person's life: "Like a dream he flies away, no more to be found" (Job 20:8). Sometimes we equate dreaming with considering possibilities and making plans. Motivational author Napoleon Hill defined a goal as "a dream with a deadline." If a dream is wedded to prayer and a God-given vision, it could result in God's blessing; but if not, it might turn into a nightmare.

Dreams and the Word of God

Dreams played an important role in many key events in Scripture, particularly in the lives of Abraham, Jacob, Joseph and Daniel; but the Bible warns us not to accept our every dream as a personal message from the Lord. Jeremiah 23:16–40 makes it clear that false prophets depend on dreams, but their dreams are but straw compared to the wheat of the Word of God. Five dreams are involved in the nativity story in Matthew 1–2 and a dream from Pilate's wife is part of the crucifixion story (Matt. 27:19). However, God's people today have the Word of God as their lamp and they can trust the Holy Spirit to teach them and guide them.

Joseph didn't own a Bible, so God spoke to him in two dreams and revealed what He was planning to do. His father pondered the dreams (Gen. 37:11) but his brothers sneered at them and hated their younger brother.

But Joseph surely must have understood that one day he would be a man of authority, and that even his family would submit to him. Because he believed God's promise, he began to "reign in life" and deal successfully with the difficult challenges that came his way.

Joseph never read Romans 5:17, but he certainly lived it! "For if, by the trespass of the one man [Adam], death reigned through that one man, how much more will those who receive God's abundant provision of grace and of the gift of righteousness reign in life through the one man, Jesus Christ!" Joseph "reigned in life" long before he put on Pharaoh's signet ring and reigned in Egypt, and this is what made him the person that he was.

The challenges that Joseph faced are still with us today. If we "reign in life" by faith as he did, we can see our God-given dreams come true. God's people have been "raised ... up with Christ and seated ... with him in the heavenly realms" (Eph. 2:6), so we are already on the throne with Jesus and *together* we reign. This means we don't have to do it alone; the Lord does it with us. What a remarkable privilege we have!

Despite all this, we live in a world which prefers to ignore God's truth and trust in lies and illusions. When we pause to consider that, we can move on to learn how Joseph turned challenges into victories and went on to rescue the Hebrew nation from destruction.

Reality versus Illusion

The late Daniel J. Boorstin wrote, "A dream is a vision or an aspiration to which we can compare reality. ... An illusion, on the other hand, is an image we have mistaken for reality." Do yourself a favor and read those statements again so you are sure you understand them. He calls Americans "the most illusioned people on earth" and warns that the "menace of unreality" is the greatest threat America faces.[1] He suggests that this "menace of unreality" has helped to create other menaces that we refuse to confront and deal with.

Joseph, the warden of the prison and Pharaoh are the only persons in the Joseph story who knew the difference between illusion and reality and acted accordingly. As for Jacob, he believed the lie his sons told him about Joseph's death, and for years the old man mourned over his "dead" son. Jacob accepted the "evidence" he saw and asked no questions; he was defeated by an illusion. His conniving sons believed that their lie would successfully solve their problems, but one fateful day, their lie was exposed by the very "dead" man they lied about.

Potiphar's wife lied to her husband about Joseph, and Potiphar believed her and put him in prison. In spite of the evidence he saw every day of Joseph's integrity and wisdom, the jailor believed Potiphar's charge and never put in a good word for his best prisoner. The chief cupbearer probably didn't believe Joseph's story about being kidnapped and therefore forgot all about him (Gen. 40:14–15, 23). Don't most prisoners have good alibis?

However, when Joseph told Pharaoh the truth about the future famine in Egypt, Pharaoh believed him and put Joseph in charge of feeding his people. Some meteorologists find it difficult to predict the weather accurately for a week to come, yet Joseph knew what would happen for the next fourteen years! "People everywhere enjoy believing things they know are not true," wrote *New York Times* drama critic Brooks Atkinson. "It spares them the ordeal of thinking for themselves and taking responsibility for what they know."[2] Read that again.

This explains why Satan, the illusionist, finds it easy to deceive people: it's easier for them to be fooled than to take time to think. "You will not certainly die" coupled with ". . . you will be like God" (Gen. 3:4–5) was an offer Eve couldn't resist. Knowing and using the Word of God, Jesus saw through the devil's cheap counterfeits. He knew they were illusions, substitutes for the promises He had already received from His Father; so He successfully resisted the enemy (Matt. 4:1–11).

Unfortunately, many Christians have adopted some of the enemy's illusions and have abandoned the truth of God's Word. "Size is a measure of success" is one such illusion, and it is unreliable whether you are measuring budgets, buildings or bodies. "To attract the world, you must imitate the world" is another one, and so is, "We have plenty of talent, we don't need prayer and the Holy Spirit." Once church leaders start believing and promoting these illusions and others like them, "righteousness stands at a distance; truth has stumbled in the streets, honesty cannot enter" (Isa. 59:14). The prophet is describing a traffic jam! And what caused it? God's people abandoning God's truth and accepting illusions. Sir Walter Scott was right:

> O what a tangled web we weave,
> When first we practice to deceive.

The first challenge Joseph had to face was family conflict, which was nothing new among the descendants of Abraham. Ishmael mocked Isaac (Gen. 21:8–10) and Esau threatened to kill Jacob (Gen. 27:41). After marrying his daughter Rachel to Jacob, Laban quarreled with him at least thirteen years, climaxing with a head-on confrontation that could have led to a free-for-all if the Lord had not intervened. Most families have their disagreements, but when it came to competition, envy and deception, Jacob's family took the prize.

Unfortunately, Jacob helped to create some of Joseph's problems because he favored the firstborn son of his beloved Rachel, the son of his old age. Jacob gave him an expensive "richly ornamented robe," the kind of garment worn by royalty and by sons who were marked out to inherit their father's wealth. It was definitely not what the young men in that day wore when they were caring for the sheep. Moreover, whenever Jacob sent Joseph out to the fields, it was to obtain up-to-date information not only about the state of the flocks but also about the conduct of his brothers, and the men knew this (Gen. 37:2, 12–36).

But Joseph unwittingly contributed to the family feud by reporting two dreams that elevated him above all the family (Gen. 37:2–12). He pictured himself and his brothers each binding sheaves in a field, and their sheaves bowed down to his sheaf. In the second dream, the sun, moon and eleven stars bowed down to him. Even his overindulging father was upset with that one.[3] On his deathbed, Jacob pictured this family conflict as a war, with the brothers shooting arrows at Joseph but not harming him (Gen. 49:22–26). Did Jacob perceive from Joseph's dream that the Lord had destined Joseph to rule?

The brothers called Joseph "the dreamer" (Gen. 37:19), implying "the dream expert" or "the dream master." Little did they realize that the fulfillment of their brother's dreams would mean deliverance for their family and the entire Jewish nation. Their attitude was, "We will not have this man to reign over us" (Luke 19:14, NKJV). In spite of Joseph's tears and pleas, they would have killed him had they not decided to sell him to Midianite merchants in a passing caravan going to Egypt (Gen. 37:12–28; 42:21–22). The brothers made some money and disposed of their troublesome brother; now all they had to do was lie to their aged father.

However, before we pass judgment on the sons of Jacob, we need to examine ourselves, our families and our churches to see what the "love quotient" really is. "Let love be without hypocrisy," wrote Paul. "Be kindly affectionate to one another with brotherly love, in honor giving preference to one another" (Rom. 12:9–10, NKJV).

Reigning through Serving

Joseph was sold as a slave to Potiphar, a high official in Pharaoh's court who may have been in charge of Pharaoh's private bodyguards. Why must this young man become a slave? One of the basic principles of "reigning in life" is learning to obey and serve faithfully, no matter who is in charge. We must begin by being servants before God can exalt us to being rulers (Matt. 25:21, 23; Phil. 2:5–11). Joseph had exchanged his beautiful coat for a servant's cloak, but Joseph's heart had not changed. Above all else he wanted to please the Lord, and the Lord not only blessed Joseph so that he was promoted, but He made Joseph a blessing to the entire household (Gen. 12:1–3). It wasn't long before Potiphar put everything into Joseph's hands.

As often happens in times of great blessing, the Enemy came and presented Joseph with his second challenge: a repeated temptation to impurity from Potiphar's deceitful and lustful wife (Gen. 39:1–19). One day she cleverly arranged to be alone with Joseph, held him by his cloak and offered herself to him. Joseph refused to sin against God, his master and himself (1 Cor. 6:18) and fled from the house, leaving his cloak behind (see 2 Tim. 2:22). When her plan failed, the woman's passion turned to hatred and she sought revenge. She lied to her husband about Joseph's conduct and Potiphar exercised his authority and put innocent Joseph into prison. Potiphar lived by illusions rather than by truth. Jacob saw blood on Joseph's garment and assumed the boy was dead. Joseph's cloak in his wife's hand convinced Potiphar that his steward had run away after his failed attempt to assault her. It's easier to build on illusions because then we don't have to think too much.

If we didn't know the rest of the Joseph story, we'd cry out, "Unfair! Unfair!" After all, it was Potiphar's wife who deserved the punishment, not Joseph; but God knows what He's doing, even though we don't always understand His ways (Isa. 55:8–9). In prison Joseph was about to face another challenge, and his victory would lead him to freedom and a throne.

Learning Patience in Prison

At the beginning of his prison sentence, Joseph suffered both emotionally and physically. "They bruised his feet with shackles, his neck was put in irons" (Ps. 105:18). Potiphar wanted to be sure this handsome young Hebrew learned his lesson, but it was God who was in charge, not Potiphar. The Lord put Joseph into prison to prepare the way for Jacob's family to move to Egypt and become a great nation (Ps. 105:17). Joseph's imprisonment would help keep the Hebrew nation alive so the Savior could be born into the world. The Lord was with Joseph and eventually the warden turned the management of the prisoners over to him. Once again, by his willingness to be a servant, Joseph became a ruler. To reign in life has little to do with the circumstances around us and everything to do with the faith and submission within us and our willingness to serve others for God's glory.

But the Lord was also at work in the palace. Pharaoh was offended by something his baker and his cupbearer had done and he sent both of them to prison, not realizing he was obeying the Lord's command. The Lord works not only in palaces but also in the minds of common people, and one night He gave both of the men dreams so disturbing that the experience robbed them of their peace. Since Joseph had a heart for people, he quickly noticed that the two men were sad, and he asked what was wrong. When he learned they were in need of interpretations for their dreams, he gave God the glory and told them what was about to happen: the chief cupbearer would be released within three days, but the baker would be executed. That's exactly what happened!

I may be wrong, but it seems that at this point that we see evidence that Joseph's patience is weakening just a bit, because he asked the cupbearer to intercede with Pharaoh on his behalf. "The chief cupbearer, however, did not remember Joseph; he forgot him" (Gen. 40:23). However, two years later, the Lord would jog the cupbearer's memory and he would tell Pharaoh about Joseph's skill at interpreting dreams. Then things would begin to happen.

The important point, however, is that God has His schedule, and we must say with David, "My times are in your hands" (Ps. 31:15). *Joseph was learning to wait on the Lord.* The ability to wait calmly for the Lord to work is one mark of the maturing believer (James 1:2–4), and those who lack patience will miss the best God has for them. Abraham, Isaac and Jacob all had to be patient and wait for God's will to be fulfilled in His time. David may have had Joseph in mind when he wrote, "Be still before the Lord and wait patiently for him; do not fret when people succeed in their ways, when they carry out their wicked schemes. . . . For those who are evil will be destroyed, but those who hope in the Lord will inherit the land" (Ps. 37:7, 9).

The Seduction of Success

Joseph is now about to enter eighty years of comfort and success (Gen. 50:22), a challenge more difficult than any he had faced so far. Most of us have no difficulty trusting the Lord when life is difficult, but when life is comfortable, we tend to take His blessings for granted and start drifting. Success can be very seductive. Charles de Gaulle said, "Success contains within it the germs of failure, and the reverse is also true."

"I have learned to be content whatever the circumstances," wrote the apostle Paul. "I know what it is to be in need, and I know what it is to have plenty" (Phil. 4:11–12). Joseph also knew both extremes and profited in his own character from them. As Moses prepared the people of Israel to enter the Promised Land, he warned them to avoid pride and self-satisfaction when they began to enjoy the riches the Lord was giving them (Deut. 8:7–20). They were to be thankful to the Lord and obey His Word; otherwise, they would forget Him and start worshiping the idols their neighbors worshiped. Israel was faithful during the rigors of war, but in times of peace and plenty, they turned away from God, and He had to discipline them.

Egyptologists tell us that a Pharaoh would occasionally sleep in a temple, hoping that the gods would give him guidance in his dreams. It makes no difference to the Lord where people sleep, because He can send dreams to anyone in any place. He sent two dreams to Pharaoh, but the Egyptian wise men could not interpret them. Then the cupbearer remembered what Joseph had done for him, and Pharaoh sent for the young prisoner. Joseph quickly bathed and changed clothes and stood before Pharaoh, who asked him to interpret his dreams. "I cannot do it," said Joseph, "but God will give Pharaoh the answer he desires" (Gen. 41:16). Like Daniel centuries later, Joseph gave all the glory to the Lord (Dan. 2:27–28). What a leader!

The time had come for Joseph's promotion. Joseph was seventeen years old when his troubles started (Gen. 37:2), and he was now thirty years old (41:46) and second ruler in the land. But those thirteen years had not been wasted, for God had used them to build Himself a man, a leader who would honor Him and do His will. As Joseph interpreted Pharaoh's two dreams, he must have recalled the two dreams God had given him thirteen years earlier, and surely he was humbled and grateful to the Lord. When we walk with God, success humbles us and we seek to use it to help others. If we aren't walking with God, success can inflate us and even destroy us.

Joseph was given a new name—Zaphenath-Paneah—which is variously translated as "God speaks and lives," "through him the living God speaks," and "he who knows things." I like Elie Wiesel's translation—"the code-breaker."[4] Fortunately, the people avoided his throne name and used his given name, including Pharaoh (Gen. 41:55).

Joseph was also given a wife who bore him two sons, and he gave them Hebrew names: Manasseh ("forgetting") and Ephraim ("twice fruitful"). These names reveal Joseph's attitude toward his past and his present. As for the past, he would not hold any grudges against his brothers because of what they did ("forgetting"). As for the present, he was determined to have a fruitful ministry in Egypt, and he did. This is a good example for us to follow when life seems to treat us unfairly.

But there was still some unfinished business involving the future. How could he get word to his father that he was alive and at the same time bring his deceitful brothers to repentance? If the brothers' sins were not dealt with, how could the Lord use them to found the nation that would bring the Savior into the world? Joseph knew that God would work everything out, because his dreams had told him so. God would give Joseph wisdom to know how to get them to face their cruelty and deception, and they would make a new beginning. It was the only way to save the nation from extinction.

Bringing His Brothers to Repentance

Perhaps the hardest challenge Joseph faced was dealing with his brothers. He exercised almost absolute authority in Egypt, but authority alone would not bring about change in the ten men who sold him and lied to their father. Joseph knew it would take time and patience for God to bring them to repentance.

When I was teaching Genesis in my radio ministry, I received a letter from a critical listener saying that Joseph was too hard on his brothers and that he should have exercised more love. Read First Corinthians 13:4–7 and judge whether Joseph's love qualifies. In dealing with his brothers, Joseph may have hurt them, *but he never harmed them!* If the men did not confess, judge their sins and forsake them, they could have no successful future. In the end, the brothers' sins were forgiven, they were reconciled to Joseph, and their father knew the truth and was rejoicing that Joseph was still alive.

No, Joseph need not apologize for putting his brothers through the difficulties of travel, leaving a "hostage" behind, bringing Benjamin to Egypt and finding the cup in the sack. They didn't realize that the harshness of the "Egyptian official" was actually an evidence of their brother's deep love for all of them. On at least three occasions, Joseph wept (32:24; 43:30; 45:14–15). But in spite of his tears, Joseph must have rejoiced when he heard Judah plead for Benjamin and offer to take his place, and when the men (speaking in Hebrew) confessed how badly they had treated Joseph. They did experience a change in heart, so Joseph's "spiritual therapy" worked.

He knew that all eleven brothers had to bow before him if the dreams were to be fulfilled and the matter be completely settled.

We can be sure that Joseph was very anxious to see Jacob and Benjamin and to gather his family together in Egypt and care for them. If there had been a better way that would take less time, he would have used it; but the Lord led him to work otherwise. Genesis 45 describes a family reconciliation unparalleled in Scripture. Joseph's explanation gave glory to the Lord, and his tears and kind words assured his brothers of his love. He gave them new clothes, provisions for the journey and carts for transporting his father and the rest of the family to Egypt.

Joseph's last words to his departing brothers are significant: "Don't quarrel on the way" (Gen. 45:24). He knew them! One would accuse the other one, this one would blame that one, and instead of enjoying a happy homecoming, their journey would be a painful funeral procession. But when Jacob saw the carts and the gifts brought home, and when he heard the words of Joseph, he became a new man. The men organized all the families, packed their household belongings and headed for Egypt, where Joseph greeted them with tears of joy.

But there was still one more problem: the brothers were unable to accept Joseph's words of assurance and feared that Joseph would punish them after their father was dead (Gen. 50:15–21). Sure enough, when the brothers returned to Egypt after burying Jacob in Canaan, they sent a message to Joseph, claiming that their father begged him to forgive their sins.

We're prone to suspect that they had fabricated the whole story, because Jacob certainly had many opportunities during those seventeen years to talk to Joseph about forgiving his brothers, and there's no record that he did. Often we impute to others what we would have done ourselves. Joseph assured them that they were forgiven and that all that had happened was a part of God's plan to save the family and the future nation. "You intended to harm me, but God intended it for good," Joseph told them (Gen. 50:20), a beautiful Old Testament version of Romans 8:28.

Learn from the Past, Learn from the Pain

Two more matters remain.

Joseph made it clear to his brothers that Egypt was not their permanent home. The Lord would fulfill His covenant with Abraham, Isaac and Jacob and take them back to their own land. He made them promise to take his body with them when they left Egypt because he wanted to be buried in the Promised Land (Gen. 50:22–26). When Israel began to face difficult times in Egypt, Joseph's coffin was a reminder to them that God cared for

His people and would not fail them. The family's promise to Joseph was passed from generation to generation, and Moses saw to it that Joseph's coffin went with them at the Exodus (Exod. 13:19). During their years of wandering in the wilderness, the presence of this coffin taught them an important lesson from the past; and after the conquest of the land, Joshua put the coffin in the family tomb, where Joseph had buried his father (Josh. 24:32; Acts 7:16; Heb. 11:22).

Imagine a dead man encouraging each new generation! People talk about "the dead past," but the past is very much alive to those who know and understand it. It's important that Christians know the past and learn from it (Heb. 11; 13:7–8). Too many congregations have amnesia and have cut themselves off from the past in their misguided desire to be "contemporary." We fix our eyes of faith on an empty cross and an empty tomb, not an ancient coffin; and our "Joseph" is alive today and interceding for us in heaven. Yes, He wants us to learn from the past; otherwise, why did He give us the inspired Scriptures?

The second matter to consider is what this experience in Egypt did for Joseph himself and what the trials of life can do for us. Psalm 105:17 tells us that God "sent a man before them," but Joseph was a teenager when he was sold in Egypt. Joseph never forgot the dreams God gave him; in the years of difficulty that followed, he became not only a man but a man of God. He was mature in faith and love, and he had wisdom beyond his years. "All inward widening is produced by outward narrowing," wrote George Matheson, and this echoes what David wrote in the psalms about his own difficult experiences. "The troubles of my heart have enlarged; bring me out of my distresses!" (Ps. 25:17 NKJV). "He also brought me out into a broad place. . . . You enlarged my path under me" (Ps. 18:19, 36 NKJV). "You have relieved [enlarged] me when I was in distress" (Ps. 4:1). Enlarged troubles should enlarge us so that we may enjoy enlarged places and paths, and do greater works for the Lord (John 14:12).

The more Joseph suffered, the more he became like Jesus. Instead of complaining, he humbled himself and became a servant, just as Jesus did (Phil. 2:5–11). Like Jesus, he was beloved of his Father (Gen. 37:3; Matt. 3:16–17) but rejected by his brethren (Gen. 37:4; John 7:1–5). Joseph was falsely accused and made a prisoner but eventually exalted to a throne! Jesus was persecuted because the leaders envied Him (Matt. 27:18), and Joseph was envied by his brothers (Gen. 37:11). The brothers conspired against him (Gen. 37:18; see Matt. 12:14), and when he was suffering, they paid no attention (Gen. 42:21; Matt. 27:27–44). I could go on, but it would be better if you meditated on the Joseph story and discovered the parallels for yourself. Of course, there are also some contrasts. Joseph suffered but he didn't die, yet Jesus gave His life for His people (Isa. 53:8), for His church (Eph. 5:25) and for individual sinners (Gal. 2:20). Joseph provided grain to *sustain* the physical lives of the people, but Jesus the Bread of Life sacrificed Himself that He might *give eternal life* to all who trust Him.

When we find ourselves in difficult circumstances, we are prone to ask, "*How* can I get out of this?" or "*When* will I get out of this?" when we should be asking, "*What* can I get out of this? Am I becoming more like the Master?"

In chapter two of his book *Up From Slavery*, Booker T. Washington writes these words of wisdom: "I have learned that success is to be measured not so much by the position that one has reached as by the obstacles which he has overcome while trying to succeed."

Joseph was an overcomer. He faced each challenge and kept moving on. His dreams divided the family and brought him suffering. His dreams also kept him going when his world seemed to be falling apart. In God's time those same dreams brought the family together and made it possible for the nation of Israel to emerge victorious from the iron furnace of Egypt.

Heaven-sent dreams lead to success; the world's illusions lead to failure.

We had better learn to tell the difference!

4

Job, the Questioner

We live on promises, not explanations.

Throughout the years of his friendship with the British essayist Samuel Johnson, James Boswell planned to write his biography; so whenever Boswell had the opportunity, he asked Johnson questions about his life. One evening, Johnson became quite upset with his young friend.

"I will not be put to the *question*," exclaimed Johnson. "Don't you consider, sir, that these are not the manners of a gentleman?"[1]

Johnson's opinion was that anyone who asked personal questions "assumed a superiority" that was quite unsociable, and perhaps Johnson was right. Unless we are giving witness in court or having a physical examination, we usually resent being pelted with questions, some of which might be too personal to answer.

God on the Witness Stand

If questioning is ungentlemanly, then nobody in the Book of Job is much of a gentleman. In the Authorized

Version, there are 329 questions in the Book of Job, including questions the Lord Himself asked. Of course, when God asks questions, He already knows the answers— but *we* don't, which is why He asks the questions. He wants to teach us. The Lord started this back in Eden when He called to Adam, "Where are you?" (Gen. 3:9). God knew where Adam was, but Adam didn't really know where he was, and that's why God called him. In Job's first speech (chap. 3), he asked "why" five times, and later in the book, he said he wanted to put God on the witness stand and question Him! Job the questioner felt qualified to cross-examine God.

But Job was a man experiencing great emotional and physical pain, and people who hurt deeply are sometimes guilty of speaking sharply. "If only my anguish could be weighed and all my misery be placed on the scales!" he lamented. "It would surely outweigh the sand of the seas— no wonder my words have been impetuous" (Job 6:2–3). Job would have been encouraged by Second Corinthians 4:17, but Paul hadn't written it yet: "For our light and momentary troubles are achieving for us an eternal glory that far outweighs them all."

But consider what caused his anguish: *in one day all his wealth was stolen or destroyed, and all his children and some of his servants were killed!* This meant that his past labors had been futile and his future dreams had been shattered. All he had was the present, and then that changed when Job lost his health and was covered with painful ulcerated sores. Unwelcomed in society, he went outside the city and sat alone on the ash heap, scraping his body with a piece of broken pottery. Whenever he fell asleep—an infrequent experience—he was terrorized by nightmares, all of which he blamed on the Lord (Job 7:14; 13:21).

His wife seemed to have little sympathy for him, or perhaps she just wanted to see him out of his agony, because she told him, "Curse God and die!" (Job 2:9). And Job's friends contributed to his pain by suggesting that he was a secret sinner and that God was punishing him. Keep in mind that Job was no ordinary citizen; he was "the greatest man among all the people of the East" (Job 1:3)! But now he was a nobody who owned nothing, a man who wished he had never been born (Job 3) and who yearned for "the good old days" when God smiled upon him and his family and friends respected him (29:1ff).

But is asking questions the best way to deal with pain?

Questions Reveal Character

It's been said that life is a school where we may not learn what the lesson was until we have flunked the examination. Sometimes this is so, but a crisis doesn't make a person; it only reveals what the person is made of. Job's mind was made up of questions. He began by taking the "intellectual" or "scientific" approach to life by insisting that God explain exactly what He was doing. But God didn't explain anything. He never told Job that Satan had declared war on Him *and that Job was the battlefield!*

The basic issue was not "Why do the righteous suffer?" but, "Is our God *in Himself* worth suffering for or are we obeying Him only because He rewards us?" Satan's challenge was, "Does Job fear God for nothing?" (Job

1:9). He accused God of paying Job to obey Him, and this was a slander against the characters of both God and Job. Satan is a clever bargainer, and once he even tried to "make a deal" with the Son of God (Matt. 4:8–11)!

There have always been professed believers who are only "commercial Christians," obeying the Lord only because there is a "payoff" at the end. What they call "salvation" is only an escape from hell, not an opportunity to serve God and enjoy heaven on earth. Not everybody is like the three Hebrew men who bravely told Nebuchadnezzar, "If the God we serve is able to deliver us, then he will deliver us from the blazing furnace and from Your Majesty's hand. *But even if he does not*, we want you to know, Your Majesty, that we will not serve your gods or worship the image of gold you have set up" (Dan. 3:17–18). These men were not bargaining; they were witnessing. Satan told God, "A man will give all he has for his own life!" (Job 2:4), but if you read your Bible and linger at Calvary, you will know that Satan was wrong.

Job was questioning what God was doing when he should have been discovering what God was like, because the purposes of God and the promises of God are both expressions of the character of God. Learning biblical theology means discovering the wonder of God's character and not just memorizing routine definitions of doctrines, as important as these definitions are. In Romans 9–11, after explaining some of the deeper mysteries of God relating to election, Paul stopped explaining and started worshiping! "Oh, the depth of the riches of the wisdom and knowledge of God! How unsearchable his judgments, and his paths beyond tracing out!" (See Rom. 11:33–36.)

"When all my attempts at exegesis fail, I worship," said G. Campbell Morgan—surely a good example for us to follow.

Certainly asking questions is a good way to learn, provided we ask the right questions in the right attitude about the right matters, things that are essential and not peripheral. However, God's people don't live on explanations; they live on promises, because God's promises reveal God's character. I was undergoing some tests at the hospital when the physician asked, "Would you like to see the inside of your stomach?" I replied, "No, I'd like to see the inside of my room." Listening to an explanation of my gastronomical environment wouldn't make me feel any better. The doctor smiled and kept probing. What I wanted to hear him say was, "I see what's wrong and we can fix it!" That's a promise, and promises produce the kind of hope you can live on!

Job needed to get better acquainted with the God he had served faithfully and, as a result, better understand himself and his critical friends. In the end the Lord rebuked the three friends for what they had said about Job and the Lord, and He commended Job for speaking truth about Him (Job 42:7–10). He told Job to intercede for his friends and He would forgive them. Imagine the humiliation of his friends when they discovered how miserably they had failed the theology test!

Job knew the promises of God and stated some of them in his conversation with his friends. However, he also knew the character of God on which those promises were founded, and this is what carried him through his painfully difficult trial. Knowing the character of God,

Job was able to turn question marks into exclamation points, and so may we when life seems to be falling apart.

The God of All Grace

When he least expected it, Job received *in one day* three rapid-fire reports of business calamities, and then a fourth report of a family catastrophe, all of which left him a bankrupt man with ten children and several servants to bury. Yet, instead of cursing God, as Satan said Job would do (Job 1:11), Job blessed the name of the LORD! "Naked I came from my mother's womb, and naked I will depart. The LORD gave and the LORD has taken away; may the name of the LORD be praised" (Job 1:21). *He found his strength in worshiping the God of sovereign grace!*

God in His grace gives us what we don't deserve, and God in His mercy doesn't give us what we do deserve. He is "the God of all grace" (1 Peter 5:10) and His grace is sufficient for every believer in every situation (2 Cor. 12:9). Three times Job used the word "LORD," which is the Hebrew word "Yahweh" or "Jehovah" and means "the self-existing God who is faithful to His covenants and His promises." Elohim (God) is His power name, but "Jehovah" (LORD) is His personal name. This is the awesome name of God that orthodox Jews revere so much that they will not speak it publicly but instead substitute the name Adonai (Lord).

Satan and Job's friends slandered Job, but God knew him best and thought very highly of him. "There is no one on earth like him; he is blameless and upright, a man who fears God and shuns evil" (Job 1:8, 2:3). God made it clear to Satan that He had permitted Job to endure all this suffering "without any reason" (Job 2:3), but, of course, Job knew nothing about the conversations in heaven. Job wasn't perfect, but he was a man of integrity and was not guilty of the accusations spoken by his friends and the devil.

"The LORD gave," said Job. In His sovereign grace, the Lord gave conception (Ps. 139:13–16) so that Job could come into the world. He equipped him to learn and to work, and He blessed his efforts so that Job became a very wealthy man. Job was also a believer who practiced his faith, was exemplary in leadership and generous in helping people in need (Job 29). His character and conduct were known by all and matched his reputation so that everybody respected him.

"The LORD has taken away." This was not an indictment against the LORD, as though He had sinned, but rather an acknowledgment of His sovereign control over all things. "But he [God] stands alone, and who can oppose him?" asked Job; and then he answered his question: "He does whatever he pleases" (23:13). The losses that Job had incurred were not coincidences or accidents but divine appointments.

The LORD also sent Job physical affliction so painful and ugly that even his wife told him he was better off dead. But Job said to his grieving wife, "Shall we accept good from God, and not trouble?" (Job 2:10). Job didn't deny the existence of evil, nor did he deny that God had permitted it. The fresh graves in the cemetery shouted "Death!" and his body shouted "Pain!" *But beyond the stark realities of pain and death, Job acknowledged the grace*

*of God and the sovereignty of God. He found in his worship
the strength to keep going.*

The God Who Never Changes

Yes, our God is gracious and sovereign. He gives
and He takes away, and we soon learn how transitory
life is and how much we need an unchanging Savior.
Our circumstances change and our feelings change, and
if we are to have stability, we need an anchor to keep
us from giving up and drifting in the rapids to ruin on
the rocks. That anchor is *hope,* and that hope is found in
the unchanging character of God. "We have this hope
as an anchor for the soul, firm and secure. It enters the
inner sanctuary [of heaven] . . . where our forerunner
Jesus has entered on our behalf (Heb. 6:19–20). Mariners
drop their anchors downward and trust they will hold,
but Christians are anchored *heavenward* where Jesus is
interceding for us, because Jesus is "our hope" (1 Tim.
1:1). We have an anchor that holds!

Our God does not change. When it comes to the
character of God and the promises based on that character,
*He cannot take away from His own people anything that
they need to glorify Him.* "I the LORD do not change" (Mal.
3:6). "Jesus Christ is the same yesterday and today and
forever" (Heb. 13:8). This truth applies to each of His
glorious attributes as well as to all His precious promises.

Job was a poor man, a grieving man, a sick man, a
man falsely accused, but he was not a godless man. He
had lost his heath, his wealth, some of his servants and all
of his children, *but he had not lost his God,* even though he
didn't fully understand all that was happening. The God

that he worshiped and served was (and is) faithful and unchanging in what He is and what He says. That's why Job was able to say, "Though he slay me, yet will I hope in him" (Job 13:15). He had confidence in the faithfulness of God, and this gave him hope.

Job's friends relied on their logical explanations, so all they could offer him was one piece of wrong advice: get right with God, and He will restore you to health and wealth. "Consider now," said Eliphaz, "who being innocent has ever perished? Where were the upright ever destroyed? As I have observed, those who plow evil and those who sow trouble reap it" (Job 4:7–8). But is this always true? I don't think so, because Scripture seems to emphasize just the opposite! In this life, the wicked seem to get away with their wicked deeds while the innocent people suffer for doing good; and the books won't be balanced until God opens them at the last judgment. David wrote about this in Psalm 37, and the sons of Korah in Psalm 49, and Asaph in Psalm 73. Jeremiah wrestled with the problem in chapter 12 of his prophecy and so did Habakkuk in the first two chapters of his book.

Few things are more hurtful than amateur theologians force-feeding hurting people with dogmatic, oversimplified explanations of what they are sure God is doing. I heard about a girl who was killed in an auto accident. When the pastor arrived, his words of comfort were: "Well, maybe the Lord knew she would grow up and become a prostitute, so He spared her that." Alas, like Job's "comforters," the pastor was a deceitful brook (Job 6:15), a worthless physician (13:14) and a miserable comforter (16:2). If we want to glorify God instead of playing God, we will comfort people and not wound them. "May the God of hope fill you with all joy and peace as you trust in him, so that you may overflow with hope by the power of the Holy Spirit" (Rom. 15:13).

For the Christian believer, "hope" is not "hope so," some kind of mysterious feeling or cloudy vision, like a child hoping for a special Christmas gift. It's much more solid than that. Consider what Paul wrote about hope in Romans 5:1–5:

> Therefore, since we have been justified through faith, we have peace with God through our Lord Jesus Christ, through whom we have gained access by faith into this grace in which we now stand. And we boast in the hope of the glory of God. Not only so, but we also glory in our sufferings, because we know that suffering produces perseverance; perseverance, character; and character, hope. And hope does not put us to shame, because God's love has been poured out into our hearts through the Holy Spirit, who has been given to us.

Hope comes from the Father and the Son and the Holy Spirit. We have hope because of salvation, because of the indwelling Spirit, and, strange as it seems, because of our suffering. Faith, hope and love combine to give us peace *with* God and the peace *of* God, as well as access into the treasury of God's inexhaustible grace; and the Holy Spirit uses all of this to build our character. What an experience! Hope generates endurance and endurance the ability to wait for God to work out His purposes in His time. "You have heard of Job's perseverance and have seen what the Lord finally brought about. The Lord is full of compassion and mercy" (James 5:11).

The God Who Refines Us

When James wrote those words, he may have been meditating on Job 23:10: "But he [God] knows the way that I take; when he has tested me, I will come forth as gold." The sovereign God of all grace is faithful and unchanging, and He loves us too much to harm us and is too wise to make a mistake. I've experienced several surgeries, and it hurts! The surgeons may have hurt me, but they did not harm me—in fact, they helped me. Two verses come to mind. Jesus said to Peter, "You do not realize now what I am doing, but later you will understand" (John 13:7). Hebrews 12:11 reminds us, "No discipline seems pleasant at the time, but painful. Later on, however, it produces a harvest of righteousness and peace for those who have been trained [exercised] by it." In times of suffering, we plant the seeds of faith and wait patiently for the harvest.

Job used several images to convey the misery of his situation, including a storm (9:17; 19:10), a war (19:11–12) and a flood (27:10); but the image of the goldsmith's furnace is perhaps the most instructive. "When he has tested me, I will come forth as gold." In spite of our natural weakness and our frequent disobedience, *we are more valuable to God than gold is to us!* Yes, we are made of clay and, if we die, our bodies will turn to dust; but until then, "we have this treasure in jars of clay to show that this all-surpassing power is from God and not from us" (2 Cor. 4:7). "I have tested you in the furnace of affliction" (Isa. 48:10). "The crucible for silver and the furnace for gold, but the Lord tests the heart" (Prov. 17:3). The furnace is not a place of lonely punishment; it's a place of divine purpose, and when we are there, God is there with us (see Dan. 3:24–27; Isa. 43:2).

When God allows His children to suffer, it's because He has a special purpose in mind, and He isn't obligated to explain that purpose to us today. In fact, we may not understand what really happened until we get to heaven and "know fully" (1 Cor. 13:12). Remember, we don't live on explanations, we live on promises; and Job 23:10 promises that our trials can refine us and bring glory to God if we will only let Him have His way. The furnace not only purifies the gold but also makes it malleable for the jeweler's hands to create something beautiful and useful.

The important thing to keep in mind is this: when the Lord puts His children into the furnace, *He keeps His eye on the clock and His hand on the thermostat!* He knows how long and how much, so we never need to fear what the future holds. Job had it right: "when he has tested me, I will come forth as gold." Why? Because God loved Job—and He loves us!

The God Who Shuts Our Mouths

Our Christian walk must always be balanced; otherwise, we'll be tottering and stumbling and going to extremes, and that's not the best way to serve God. If we focus only on the intellect, we'll have no burning heart; but if everything is emotional, we'll have zeal without knowledge. Worship must be balanced with service and receiving with giving. We need times alone and times for fellowship. So the book closes with Job discovering balance.

We've been reminded in the Book of Job that our God exercises sovereign grace, that He is faithful and that He is a loving Father. Whether we are in the midst of the battle or in the furnace, God is there with us, speaking to us from His Word. Charles Haddon Spurgeon said, "The promises of God never shine so brightly as in the furnace of affliction." I am certainly grateful for the promises God has given me during my furnace experiences!

Throughout the discussion recorded in chapters 3 through 37, the LORD has said nothing. As soon as Elihu stopped speaking, the LORD spoke and God told Job to listen because it was time for Him to ask the questions! He asked Job over fifty questions, the last one being, "Will the one who contends with the Almighty correct him?" (Job 40:2). What was Job's response? "I am unworthy—how can I reply to you? I put my hand over my mouth. I spoke once, but I have no answer—twice, but I will say no more" (Job 40:3–5).

Silence! God had shut Job's mouth! "I had a million questions to ask God," wrote Christopher Morley, "but when I met Him, they all fled my mind; and it didn't seem to matter."[2]

Then God asked Job even more questions, and that put an end to all discussion. "My ears had heard of you," said Job, "but now my eyes have seen you. Therefore I despise myself and repent in dust and ashes" (Job 42:5–6). Once by faith we get a glimpse of our awesome God and grasp but a corner of His majesty, we must submit to Him because nothing else really matters. We shut our mouths and open our hearts, and the pieces of the puzzle begin to fall into place. We begin to have clearer discernment of His love and care and we finally accept those mysteries that have disturbed us.

Have you ever met some of the people in the Bible whose mouths were shut by God? (Now *I'm* asking questions!) For instance, Joseph's brothers were speechless when they discovered that the man they had been dealing with in Egypt was their brother (Gen. 45:1–3). On several occasions Moses asked God to permit him to enter the Promised Land, and God finally shut his mouth about the matter (Deut. 3:26). David had been silent because God had shut his mouth (Ps. 39:1–3, 9), but then he spoke and cried out for God's blessing. There will come a time when all the earth will be silent before the throne of God and justice will be meted out (Hab. 2:20; Ps. 107:42). Jesus spoke about a wedding guest whose mouth was shut because he wasn't properly dressed to attend the feast (Matt. 22:12–13).

In fact, nobody can open his or her mouth in praise to God until first they have been convicted of sin and shut their mouths. It means not defending or promoting ourselves but submitting by faith to Jesus Christ. Conviction must come before conversion and silence before salvation and song. "Now we know that whatever the law says, it says to those who are under the law, so that every mouth may be silenced and the whole world held accountable to God" (Rom. 3:19).

Has your mouth ever been shut by God? Have you ever argued with Him and challenged Him, insisting that He explain everything to you? To my shame, I've been there more than once, and I had to submit to Him and let Him lovingly close my mouth. Then I had to bow in silent adoration and then get up and praise Him and obey Him. God always gives His best to those who leave the choice with Him. Solomon wrote that there is "a time to be silent and a time to speak" (Eccles. 3:7), and blessed are those believers who know what time it is!

The God of Mystery

During his time of suffering and sorrow, Job had been reminded that God is gracious and sovereign, faithful and trustworthy, loving and patient, and awesome and mysterious; and this experience brought him to the place of repentance. "Surely I spoke of things I did not understand, things too wonderful for me to know," he confessed (42:3). It's a high and holy hour in our Christian walk when we accept what we cannot explain and bow in worship before the God who manifests His attributes but still remains mysterious in His person and His works. We can't explain Him, but we know we can trust Him.

"The secret things belong to the LORD our God, but the things revealed belong to us and to our children forever, that we may follow all the words of this law" (Deut. 29:29). Obedience to what we already know is the secret of accepting and perhaps unlocking some of the mysteries that puzzle us. Jesus said, "Anyone who chooses to do the will of God will find out whether my teaching comes from God" (John 7:17). J. Sidlow Baxter said it perfectly: "The Word of God is as wise in its *reservations* as it is wonderful in its *revelations*. Enough is revealed to make faith intelligent. Enough is reserved to give faith scope for development."[3] Obedience is the first step toward knowing God and His will. "What shall I do, Lord?" (Acts 22:10) takes precedence over "What are you doing, Lord?"

Job's first statement after God's second speech was "I know you can do all things; no purpose of yours can be thwarted" (Job 42:2). God can do all things and what He does is purposeful; therefore, we can claim Romans 8:28: "And we know that in all things God works for the good of those who love him, who have been called according to his purpose." His purpose is that we might "be conformed to the image of his Son" (Rom. 8:29). Jesus endured suffering far greater than what Job experienced or that we experience today, and because He did, we shall be like Him forever (1 John 3:1–3)!

Yes, God can do anything. He has a perfect plan and the power to execute that plan. If He doesn't heal us or improve our circumstances as we think He should, it isn't because He's too weak or too ignorant of the situation. He doesn't explain every detail to us, nor is it necessary that He do so. One of the delights of heaven will be watching our lives reviewed and understanding for the first time what happened to us and why it happened. "Now I know in part; then I shall know fully, even as I am fully known" (1 Cor. 13:12).

The Book of Job closes on a happy note: Job was healed of all his afflictions, his friends apologized for their harsh criticisms, he and his wife had ten more children, his wealth was doubled and he lived to a very old age. It doesn't happen this way for everybody who suffers, because some suffer and die and are forgotten; but that it happened to Job is an assurance to us that our loving heavenly Father writes the last chapter for each life. God will see to it that the scars will become medals, the tears will become jewels, the crosses will become crowns and the sufferings of each day will glorify God forever.

What more could we ask for?

5

Moses, the Deliverer

Freedom must lead to maturity.

Remember John Godfrey Saxe's poem about the six blind men and the elephant?

Each man touched a different part of the elephant's body and confidently announced what the creature was. One touched the elephant's side and said an elephant was a wall, and another felt a tusk and said an elephant was a spear. The one who felt the trunk said it was a snake, and the man who embraced a leg declared it was a tree. To the fifth man, holding one of the elephant's ears, the elephant was a fan; and the sixth man, grasping the tail, called the elephant a rope. The elephant was just too much for them!

That's the way I feel about Moses: there is just too much of him! In the Hebrew Bible Moses is mentioned 762 times and 80 times in the Greek New Testament, a total of 842 references; and that's a lot to get your hands on. Moses was a gifted leader and a wise legislator, but he was also a husband and father, a brother, a teacher, a mentor, a man of prayer, an organizer and a great man of faith. God called him "Moses my servant" (Num. 12:7–8; Josh. 1:2).

An Amazing Life

Moses spent his first forty years as a brilliant student
in Egypt, probably being groomed to be the next pharaoh
(Acts 7:22). For the next forty years he was a fugitive and
a humble shepherd in Midian. At God's command he
returned to Egypt, delivered Israel from bondage and for
forty years led them from place to place in the wilderness.
After 120 years of faithful service to the Lord and His
people, Moses ascended Mount Nebo where he died and
the Lord buried him in an unmarked grave (Deut, 34:1–
6). For Christians today Moses lives in the Word of God,
and his inspired words point us to Jesus Christ. "If you
believed Moses, you would believe me," said Jesus, "for he
wrote about me" (John 5:46).

But life wasn't easy for Moses. When he was a newborn
baby, he was in jeopardy because Pharaoh had ordered all
male Hebrew babies to be drowned in the Nile River.
While defending a persecuted Hebrew slave, he killed the
Egyptian foreman and had to flee to Midian, where he
became a shepherd. Forty years later, God sent him back
to Egypt and helped him deliver Israel from slavery and
start them on their journey to the Promised Land. But at
Kadesh Barnea the Jews refused to enter the Promised
Land, so God made them wander in the wilderness.

Those were very difficult years for Moses, and more
than once he felt like quitting. (Read Psalm 106 for a
summary of what the Lord and Moses had to endure
from Jacob's descendants.) The people complained about
the way Moses led them and fed them, while at the
same time they were secretly worshiping the idols they
had brought from Egypt. Various tribal leaders opposed

Moses' leadership and even threatened to stone him. The people disobeyed God and then blamed Moses for the painful consequences. Twice God offered to wipe out the Israelites and build a greater nation from Moses, but he rejected both offers (Exod. 32:1–10; Num. 14:1–12). The Lord called them "a stiff-necked people" (Exod. 32:9; 33:3, 5), and Moses agreed with Him (Exod. 34:9; Deut. 31:27); yet Moses still loved them, interceded for them and yearned to see them obey the Lord and enjoy His blessings.

What kept Moses serving the Lord even when everything and everybody seemed against him? My answer may seem simplistic, but I think it's the best answer: Moses was a man who lived *for* God and *in* God. Psalm 90 is the only psalm attributed to Moses, and in the first verse he states it plainly: "Lord, you have been our dwelling place throughout all generations."

Different Locations, Same Address

After Israel's rebellion at Kadesh Barnea, Moses and his people spent the next thirty-eight years (Deut. 2:14) traveling from place to place in the wilderness, finally ending up on the plains of Moab at the border of Canaan. According to Numbers 33, between Rameses in Egypt and Mount Nebo in Moab, the Israelites relocated at least forty times! *But in all these changes, Moses maintained the same spiritual address—the LORD God Jehovah!* No matter where he and his people pitched their tents, Moses had God as his dwelling place. "Lord, you have been our dwelling place throughout all generations" is the Old Testament equivalent of what Jesus said in John 15:5. "I am the vine, you are the branches; he who abides in Me and I in him, he bears much fruit, for apart from Me you can do nothing" (NASB). When we abide in Jesus, God becomes our dwelling place, and this means we can be fruitful for the Lord.

Moses knew God personally. He heard Him speak, he saw His glory and he often cried out to Him for help and God answered. He knew God's name and God's character and had the privilege of interceding for God's people. "The LORD would speak to Moses face to face, as one speaks to a friend" (Exod. 33:11). At the end of a day's march, when the camp was quiet, Moses would lie down in his tent and know that he was safe in the arms of the Lord God. Perhaps the last words he would speak would be, "Lord, here we are in a new place; but You are still our dwelling place and will be throughout all generations." Moses didn't have to count sheep in order to go to sleep—he had counted enough of them in Midian! He just rested in the loving arms of the Shepherd.

My wife and I have traveled a good deal in our ministry. We have lived in hotels and motels, private homes and missionary guest houses, college dormitories and "prophet's chambers" in local church buildings. Some of these facilities were very adequate while others were less than sensational, but it made little difference. At the close of a demanding day of travel and ministry, we could always put our heads on our pillows knowing that we were resting in the Lord, our unchanging dwelling place. The words of David were very meaningful to us: "In peace I will lie down and sleep, for you alone, LORD, make me dwell in safety" (Ps. 4:8).

Each time the camp of Israel was being set up, Moses pitched a special "tent of meeting" outside the camp where he could be alone with God or meet with people who needed his help (Exod. 33:7–11). Please note that this "tent of meeting" was not the tabernacle, because the tabernacle was set up in the middle of the camp. Moses knew the value of solitude and "taking time to be holy." Even Jesus slipped away from the crowds to spend time alone with His Father, and this is a good example for us to follow (Matt. 14:22–23; Mark 1:35–39; Luke 4:42 and 5:16).

A pastor friend used to warn me, "Beware of the barrenness of a busy life." Each of us needs a special time and place every day to meet with our Father, to listen to His counsel from the Word, to thank Him and worship Him, and to share our concerns with Him. When we ignore this daily time, we start to depend on ourselves, and we forget that without Christ we "can do nothing" (John 15:5). We are not just handicapped; we are helpless.

Moses was "educated in all the wisdom of the Egyptians" (Acts 7:22), but that wasn't the secret of his success or his remarkable endurance as a leader. I'm grateful for books, classes and teachers, and I've profited from every school I've attended. But I must confess that what God has taught me from His Word is what has carried us through in our ministry. There is no evidence that the wisdom of Egypt helped Moses in his spiritual ministry to Israel. Like Moses, the apostle Paul was a highly educated man, and, like Moses, he knew the difference between the wisdom of this world and the wisdom of God (1 Cor. 1:18–31). The knowledge of facts and methods is one thing, and the understanding and applying of spiritual truths is quite something else. God "made known his ways unto Moses, his deeds to the people of Israel" (Ps. 103:7). The people could see *what* God was doing, but Moses had the spiritual insight to know *why* God was doing it. Moses didn't learn that in Egypt. He learned God's ways from listening to God's words.

People who know *how* to do things will always have jobs, and the people who know *why* things are done that way will always be their bosses. Leaders are people who have the wisdom that comes from humility, experience and insight. The wisdom of Egypt may have stimulated Moses' mind, but the wisdom of God instructed his heart and opened his eyes to see God's truth. "The fear of the LORD is the beginning of knowledge" (Prov. 1:7).

It's likely that Moses learned more about God and the realities of life while caring for his father-in-law's sheep in Midian than he did while preparing his class assignments in Egypt. By nature sheep are stubborn animals with a tendency to want their own way, and caring for them helped to prepare Moses to lead the people of Israel— *who frequently behaved just like stubborn sheep!*

Our son, a pastor, stopped to visit a church member on his farm as the man was trying to put some sheep where they belonged. "I tell you," the frustrated farmer said, "sheep are the dumbest creatures God ever made!" Sometimes God's people can be just as stubborn. It's not an accident that both Jesus and Paul joined Moses, David and Isaiah in comparing people to sheep.

So what do we do with these sheep? We do all we can to help them grow up.

The Slave Mentality

Taking the Hebrews out of Egypt was not the greatest challenge Moses faced. That miracle was accomplished in one night. The greatest challenge Moses faced was *taking Egypt out of the Hebrews*. To accomplish this an entire generation had to die so that a new generation could take over. The older generation had been slaves for so long that they had forgotten the meaning of freedom. They had grown so accustomed to the small certainties of their Egyptian bondage that they had forgotten the big things God had done for them and had promised them. They were content to sacrifice their precious freedom in exchange for shelter, food and a certain amount of security. It didn't enter their minds that they had been destined by God to be a free people and a great people, serving the Lord in their own land. As Paul teaches in Romans 6, the "old" must die before we can enter into "newness of life."

Moses knew that there was a deeper problem than just Israel's enslavement to the Egyptians. *The people of Israel were enslaved to their own appetites.* All the Egyptians had to do was satisfy those desires and the Hebrews were under their control. The Israelites had a "slave mentality" and were willing to sacrifice liberty and identity in return for security and sensuality. Trace Israel's trek through the wilderness and note how often the people contrasted their "difficult circumstances" as a free people with the "good times" they had enjoyed in Egypt as slaves. Egypt wasn't such a terrible place after all! Listen to them:

> If only we had died by the Lord's hand in Egypt! There we sat around the pots of meat and ate all the food we wanted, but you [Moses] have brought us out into this desert to starve this entire assembly to death. (Exod. 16:3)

> Why did you bring us up out of Egypt to make us and our children and livestock die of thirst? (Exod. 17:3)

> If only we had meat to eat! We remember the fish we ate in Egypt at no cost—also the cucumbers, melons, leeks, onions and garlic. But now we have lost our appetite; we never see anything but this manna! (Num. 11:4–6)

> If only we had died in Egypt. Or in this wilderness! (Num. 14:2)[1]

> Why did you bring the Lord's community into this wilderness, that we and our livestock should die here? Why did you bring us up out of Egypt to this terrible place? It has no grain or figs, grapevines or pomegranates. And there is no water to drink! (Num. 20:4–5)

How tragic that the people thought that slavery in Egypt was ecstasy but that freedom to follow the Lord to the Promised Land was misery! This is what Scripture calls "sin's deceitfulness" (Heb. 3:13). They thought they were free when they were actually in great bondage. Egypt had so captured and controlled their appetites that the Hebrews didn't know the difference, and all the while they were becoming more and more enslaved to their own appetites.

Moses had to teach the nation of Israel what parents must teach their children, and what pastors must teach their congregations, that loving obedience to authority is the royal route to joy and true freedom. To be controlled by our appetites is a terrible form of servitude. God asks for our obedience, not to make us slaves but to help us become free. His commands are invitations for us to enter into a deeper relationship of liberty and love, for "his commands are not burdensome" (1 John 5:3).

One obvious evidence of immaturity is fear. Children fear thunder and lightning, shadows in the night and strange sounds in the dark. Israel had seen the Lord demonstrate His great power as He devastated the land of Egypt, yet the people stood trembling at the Red Sea, afraid of the approaching Egyptian army. "They said to Moses, "Was it because there were no graves in Egypt that you brought us to the desert to die" What have you done to us by bringing us out of Egypt? Didn't we say to you in Egypt, 'Leave us alone; let us serve the Egyptians'? It would have been better for us to serve the Egyptians than to die in the desert!"(Exod. 14:11–12).

Of course, children need to have a healthy fear of some things, such as moving vehicles, and so we teach them to look both ways before crossing a street. We must explain the dangers of poison, electricity, sharp tools, heights and cunning people. But these are fears that *energize* us rather than *paralyze* us. When they appear, they mobilize us to act quickly and get out of the danger zone. When we love the Father and obey His will, we have nothing to fear. "There is no fear in love. But perfect [mature] love drives out fear" (1 John 4:18).

Anyone who has raised a family knows that complaining and blaming others are common faults of young children (and many adults). You leave on a vacation trip, stop at the first traffic light, and someone always asks, "Are we there yet?" The weather is always too hot or too cold. The food isn't fun to eat. Junior got a bigger ice cream cone than his sister.

The people of Israel were no different. Every time there was a crisis in their journey, they acted like children in a playpen instead of warriors on a battlefield. They didn't turn to the Lord and pray; they ran to Moses and blamed him. "Do everything without grumbling and arguing" (Phil. 2:14) is still in God's Word, and that word "everything" challenges us.

We expect children to say and do childish things because they lack experience and haven't been around long enough to profit from history. Israel had a wonderful history that would encourage them in any situation, *but they repeatedly forgot it!* "Our ancestors in Egypt were not impressed by the Lord's miraculous deeds. They soon forgot his many acts of kindness to them" (Ps. 106:7; see also vv. 13, 21). In his farewell message recorded in Deuteronomy, Moses reviewed Israel's past and frequently exhorted the people to remember what God had done and said. Philosopher George Santayana may have been thinking of Israel when we wrote, "Those who do not remember the past are condemned to relive it." Israel is exhibit A of this aphorism, as you will discover if you read the Book of Judges.

The Road to Maturity

There's a vast difference between *growing old* (aging) and *growing up* (maturing). Unless a child suffers from neglect or a crippling affliction, he or she will grow up physically to become an adult; but not every adult matures psychologically, socially or spiritually. Such problems as spousal abuse, child abuse, road rage and chronic unemployment are often signs of emotional immaturity. Immature people in mature bodies can be as dangerous as land mines and often as difficult to defuse.

How did the Lord encourage His people to mature as they made their way to the Promised Land? He challenged their faith by putting them through various trials, because obedience and patience in trials will help produce maturity (James 1:2–8). The Lord didn't allow Israel to use any shortcuts as they began their march; instead, He led them "in a roundabout way" (Exod. 13:17–18).Ultimately, shortcuts usually turn out to be longer and more difficult than the main road. This gave the Egyptians opportunity to pursue them until Israel was trapped (Exod. 14:1–14). *But trusting the Lord in "impossible" situations is what builds our faith and glorifies the Lord!* God opened up the sea and the Israelites crossed over on dry land. Then the Lord closed up the sea and the Egyptian army drowned (Exod. 14:15–31).

But other trials awaited the people of Israel: thirst (Exod. 15:22–27), hunger (Exod. 16), more thirst (Exod. 17:1–7) and military attack (Exod. 17:8–15). Maturing Christians don't complain but are patient and trusting in times of testing, knowing that trials are appointments and not accidents, disciplines and not punishments, and that our heavenly Father is able to meet every need.

When Israel came to Mount Sinai, they camped there for about two years (Num. 10:11). There was food to eat and water to drink, and there were no enemy attacks. What, then, were they doing there? For one thing, Moses was supervising the making of the tabernacle, the ordaining of the priests and the establishing of the sacrificial system. This would teach the people about the grace of God as well as God's hatred of sin. From that time forth, the tabernacle would be at the center of the camp with the glory cloud hovering over it. The children of Israel also learned to give generously to the Lord, because the materials for the tabernacle were contributed by the people (Exod. 25:1–7; 35:4–29).

The clouds, thunder and lightning on Mount Sinai would convey the grandeur and majesty of God. The voice of God speaking and giving Moses His holy law would help to instill in the people the fear of the Lord. Sinai was Israel's "school" for learning how to submit to God's authority, appreciate His character and respect His Word. *There can be no true maturity in our lives until we have learned to submit to authority.* "The first duty of every soul," wrote theologian P. T. Forsyth, "is to find not its freedom but its Master."[2] That Master is Jesus Christ, who said, "Take my yoke upon you and learn from me, for I am gentle and humble in heart, and you shall find rest for your souls. For my yoke is easy and my burden is light" (Matt. 11:29–30).

At Mount Sinai Israel saw the glory of God, received the law of God and entered into a covenant with God to fear Him and obey Him. They began to understand the sinfulness of man and the grace of God in His willingness to forgive. They also began to realize that all of life must be sanctified and used for His glory. Whether in their personal decisions, their families, their daily work or their relationships with others, they must live to please God. The freedom God gave them was not an occasional thing, like a holiday, but a total life experience that carried responsibilities as well as privileges.

Finally, they were reminded by their calendar of feasts (Lev. 23) to remember and understand the past and acknowledge what God had done for them. We are all standing on the shoulders of giants, and historical amnesia is one of the worst things that can happen to an individual, a family, a church or a nation. To know the past is to be inspired by the best that happened, warned by the worst that happened and cautioned to be prepared by what might happen again. Ignoring the past could mean wasting the opportunities of the present and destroying the possibilities of the future.

Leading Others into Maturity

God had to mature Moses and equip him to be able to lead Israel into maturity, and Moses never stopped growing in the grace of God and the knowledge of God. We can never lead others where we haven't been ourselves, and if we try to pretend we can, the masquerade will eventually be revealed.

Moses had comfort and honor in the palace, but these experiences didn't harden his heart against his own people. The arrogant opposition of Pharaoh—"Who is the Lord that I should serve him?"—didn't frighten Moses into compromise. It's difficult enough to lead a few children in our homes into maturity, but just think of doing that for an entire nation! No leader is perfect, including Moses; but some live closer to God than do others and accomplish remarkable things by the power of God.

The apostle Paul compared the maturing of believers to the birth of a baby (Gal. 4:19) and even to a wrestling match!

> My dear children, for whom I am again in pains of childbirth until Christ is formed in you ... (Gal. 4:19)

> We proclaim him [Christ], admonishing and teaching everyone with all wisdom, so that we may present everyone fully mature in Christ. To this end I strenuously contend [agonize] with all the energy Christ so powerfully works in me. I want you to know how hard I am contending [agonizing] for you and for those at Laodicea, and for all who have not met me personally. My goal is that they may be encouraged in heart and united in love, so that they may have the full riches of complete understanding, in order that they may know the mystery of God, namely, Christ, in whom are hidden all the treasures of wisdom and knowledge. (Col. 1:28–29; 2:1–3)

Note Paul's vocabulary: "I am again in pains," "I strenuously contend ... how hard I am contending." This doesn't sound like a brief Bible study followed by a video, served with tea and toast! The focus of his ministry was on Christ, and the goal of his ministry was the kind of spiritual maturity that enabled the believers to enter into the full riches of Christ in their daily lives. He wanted them to be enriched, united in Christ and encouraged in Christ, so he prayed for them and shared with them the truth of the Scriptures.

Fortunately, the believers at Colosse had Epaphras as their shepherd, "a servant of Christ Jesus . . . always wrestling [agonizing] in prayer for you, that you may stand firm in all the will of God, mature and fully assured. I vouch for him that he is working hard for you and for those at Laodicea and Hieropolis" (Col. 4:12–13). There are times when our praying is calm and more like two friends sharing their hearts, but there are also times when prayer is a struggle, a wrestling match with God or with the Enemy. (If you want more information about "wrestling in prayer," read Genesis 32:22–32 and Daniel 9.)

How many times Moses met God on the mountain, or in the tent of meeting, and interceded for the people he loved! How many times he had to listen to their foolish accusations and complaints, the "baby talk" of immature people who wanted to act important. How pained he must have been when he heard their repeated chant, "Back to Egypt! Back to Egypt! Let's choose a new leader and go back to Egypt!" Little did these rebels know that, were it not for Moses' intercession, God would have killed them.

They falsely accused him, disobeyed him, lied to him and often broke his heart, but Moses didn't quit. God used him to bring freedom to the Hebrew people and to lead a younger generation into maturity. When Joshua took over the leadership, the people were ready to fight the enemy and claim their inheritance.

In his book *Working and Thinking on the Waterfront*, the longshoreman/philosopher Eric Hoffer wrote, "Moses wanted to turn a tribe of enslaved Hebrews into free men. You would think that all he had to do was gather the slaves and tell them they were free. But Moses knew better. He knew that the transformation of slaves into free men was more difficult and painful than the transformation of free men into slaves."[3]

But first God had to transform Moses into a maturing leader.

And Moses allowed the Lord to do it, and Moses didn't give up!

6

Ruth, the Resolver

Decision and determination influence destiny.

In my own daily Bible reading, I'm always happy to complete the Book of Judges. That's the book that tells us about people who "do their own thing" and therefore make a mess of their own lives and God's world. It's refreshing to move into the Book of Ruth and go to Bethlehem where life is safer and saner. The Book of Judges reminds me of our modern society with its rivalries, atrocities and fantasies; but in Ruth we meet the basics of life, like birth and death, labor and food, joy and sorrow, loneliness and love, sacrifice and service. Nobody masquerades in the Book of Ruth, because they have the courage to refuse the artificial and devote themselves to the authentic.

Ruth, the heroine of the book, is one of the finest women found anywhere in the Bible or on the pages of secular literature. When it comes to godly decision and determination, she ranks with Rebekah, Deborah, Hannah and Mary, the mother of our Lord. She knew when to say no and when to say yes, and she knew how to stand resolutely by her decisions. She knew what it meant to work hard and get tired; to forget herself and care for others; and when she had done her best, she knew how to sit still and let the Lord work everything out. She endured more pain in a few short years than many people do in a lifetime, including the death of her husband and relocation to a strange land whose citizens would likely treat her as an enemy. She faced one difficulty after another, but Ruth didn't quit.

This little book is in the Bible, not only because Ruth is a marvelous example of endurance, but because of the important part she played in God's great plan of salvation. Ruth married Boaz and God gave them a son—Obed, who became the father of David, Israel's greatest king. Mary and Joseph were both "of the house and line of David" (Luke 2:4), and it was through Mary that our Savior Jesus Christ came into the world. Ruth is one of five women mentioned in Matthew's genealogy of Jesus (Matt. 1:3, 5–6, 16), and Jewish people didn't usually mention the mothers when they wrote the family tree. Thanks to Ruth, Tamar, Rahab, Bathsheba and Mary, I have a Savior!

I want to focus on three spiritual experiences in Ruth's life that helped her endure trials and accomplish God's will.

Great Faith

Let's begin with *her great experience of faith* in the true and living God. We can say of her what Jesus said of the Canaanite woman, "Woman, you have great faith" (Matt. 15:28).

Ruth was born into a Moabite family, and Moses had commanded, "No Ammonite or Moabite or any of their descendants may enter the assembly of the LORD, not even in the tenth generation" (Deut. 23:3). But when famine came to Judah, Elimelech and Naomi and their two sons abandoned Bethlehem ("the house of bread") and went to Moab, intending to live there only "for a while" (Ruth 1:1). Commenting on their decision, Charles Spurgeon said, "Better poverty with the people of God, than plenty outside of the covenanted land." But although they ignored God's law, He overruled their decisions and brought blessing in spite of their disobedience.

We don't know how long the family lived in Moab before Elimelech died, but we get the impression it was after his death that the two boys got married to Moabite women, contrary to the law of God (Neh. 13:1–3). The Moabites worshiped Chemosh (Num. 21:29; Jer. 48:46), one of the worst of the pagan gods (1 Kings 11:7), whose priests sacrificed little children on the altar (Lev. 20:1–5). Ten years later, the two brothers died, and Naomi was left with her daughters-in-law, Orpah and Ruth.

News came to Moab that the famine in Judah had ended, so Naomi started off for Bethlehem with her two daughters-in-law. But early in the journey, she decided to go it alone and urged Orpah and Ruth to return home. Surely she knew the pagan darkness that enshrouded the people, but she argued that she was too old to have any more sons for them to wed. Perhaps she didn't want her friends in Bethlehem to know that her sons had married heathen wives. At first both of them insisted on continuing with Naomi, but then Orpah yielded, kissed her mother-in-law goodbye and turned back to Moab. She is heard of no more in Scripture.

But there was no turning back for Ruth! Her testimony is one of the greatest confessions of faith recorded in Scripture, ranking with those of Job (23:10), Joshua (24:15), Peter (Matt. 16:16) and Paul (2 Tim. 1:12):

> Don't urge me to leave you or to turn back from you. Where you go I will go, and where you stay I will stay. Your people will be my people and your God my God. Where you die I will die, and there I will be buried. May the LORD deal with me, be it ever so severely, if even death separates you and me. (Ruth 1:16–17)

"I am going with you, no matter where you go," she said, and she meant it. "I will stay with you, no matter where you stay, because I want to belong to your people. I have abandoned my dead idols and now believe in the true and living God. If you die before I do, I will care for your grave; and when I die, I will be buried next to you, so death will not separate us. Because we both believe in the LORD God and He has accepted us, we will be together with Him forever!"

How did this saving faith come to the heart of this remarkable woman? To be sure, "Salvation comes from the LORD" (Jon. 2:9) and saving faith is a gracious gift from God (Acts 11:17; Eph. 2:8–9); but there had to be some kind of witness given that God could use to open her eyes and touch her heart. I think it was the quiet witness of Naomi, especially when Elimelech died and then her two sons. Naomi sorrowed, but not like one who had no hope. There in Moab, Naomi may not have been in the center of God's will, but still she gave enough of a loving witness that Ruth saw the reality of her mother-in-law's faith and "turned to God from idols to serve the living and true God" (1 Thess. 1:9).

Ruth's glorious experience of saving faith was later described by Boaz in these words: "May you be richly rewarded by the LORD, the God of Israel, under whose wings you have come to take refuge" (Ruth 2:12). I don't think Boaz was referring here to a mother hen protecting her chicks (Matt. 23:37) but rather to the wings of the cherubim over the ark in the Holy of Holies of the tabernacle (Exod. 25:10–22). Ruth was now over-shadowed and protected by the glory of God! David wrote, "How priceless is your unfailing love, O God! People take refuge in the shadow of your wings. They feast on the abundance of your house; you give them drink from your river of delights." (Ps. 36:7–8) Instead of going back to the old life, by faith Ruth had gone into the Holy of Holies to "rest in the shadow of the Almighty" (Ps. 91:1). The rejected woman of Moab, shut out from Israel by the law of God, was now accepted and welcomed because of God's grace and mercy.

The ways of God are past finding out. A disobedient Hebrew family doubts God's care and forsakes "the house of bread" for the land of idols. The three men in the family die, which may have been God's discipline, and one daughter-in-law returns to her parental home. But Ruth gives her heart to the true and living God because of the witness of Naomi, and Ruth eventually becomes the grandmother of David, the king of Israel! From David's family the Savior was born.

Great Hope

But Ruth's faith was just the beginning of her wonderful new life, because that great experience of faith brought with it *a greater experience of hope!*

Had Ruth never met Naomi, she might not have heard about the true and living God and the salvation He offers to those who will repent and believe. Ruth's situation in Moab was hopeless; Paul described it in Ephesians 2:12: "separate from Christ, excluded from citizenship in Israel and foreigners to the covenants of promise, without hope and without God in the world."

God never promised to raise up a Savior from Moab, because "salvation is from the Jews" (John 4:22). The law of God excluded the Moabites from Jewish citizenship (Deut. 3:3–6), and the Lord never made a covenant with Moab as He did with Israel. The gods of Moab were false gods, so the people were "without God in the world." It all added up to "without hope."

Hope is what keeps people going. Not "hope so," which is only a gallant attempt to work up happy feelings that distract us from our troubles, but real hope that is based on the character and the promises of God. Christians can endure times of trouble and even profit from them because we are "inspired by hope in our Lord Jesus Christ" (1 Thess. 1:3). Peter calls it "a living hope" because it's centered in the living Christ (1 Peter 1:3). Dead hopes fade and die because they are rooted in weak human words and works, but the Christian's hope is rooted in the living Christ and His living Word. Paul knew the difference when he prayed, "May the God of hope fill you with all joy and peace as you trust in him, so that you may overflow with hope by the power of the Holy Spirit" (Rom. 15:13).

Ruth was now a part of a new fellowship—"a chosen people, a royal priesthood, a holy nation, God's special possession" (1 Peter 2:9). She had made a new beginning through faith and was now on her way to a new home and a new future. Little did she realize that God would use her as one of the "living links" to bring the Savior into the world.

As she and Naomi made their way to Bethlehem, Ruth must have been anticipating what she would experience there; and as the children of God, we should live "in the future tense" just like the apostle Paul. "Forgetting what is behind and straining toward what is ahead, I press on toward the goal to win the prize for which God has called me heavenward in Christ Jesus" (Phil. 3:13–14). Too often we rob ourselves of joy by brooding over past mistakes and sins, when we should be focusing on what God has done for us and what He has promised for our future. When Satan the accuser attacks us (Rev. 12:10; Zech. 3), we must turn to Jesus Christ our Advocate whose sacrifice on the cross has once for all defeated the devil (1 John 2:1–2; Col. 1:13–14). "Their sins and lawless acts I will remember no more" is God's guarantee (Heb. 10:17), so why should we remember what God has forgotten?

Great Love

The miracles in Ruth's life began with a great experience of faith that led to an even greater experience of hope; but when she arrived in Bethlehem, she discovered *the greatest experience of love.* "And now these three remain: faith, hope and love. But the greatest of these is love" (1 Cor. 13:13). Ruth is a beautiful illustration of what Paul wrote in Romans 5:1–5 about every true Christian believer:

> Therefore, since we have been justified [declared righteous] through faith, we have peace with God through our Lord Jesus Christ, through whom we have gained access by faith into this grace in which we now stand. And we boast in the hope of the glory of God. Not only so, but we also glory in our sufferings, because we know that suffering produces perseverance; perseverance, character; and character, hope; And hope does not put us to shame, because God's love has been poured out into our hearts through the Holy Spirit who has been given to us.

Faith—hope—*love!*
Perseverance—character—hope—*love!*

The story of Ruth is fundamentally a love story. Because God loved Ruth, He brought her to Himself in saving faith. "This is love: not that we loved God, but that he loved us and sent his Son as an atoning sacrifice for our sins. . . . We love because he first loved us" (1 John 4:10, 19). In love He gave her the companionship of Naomi; and through Naomi, she had the promise of a husband because of the Levitical law of the kinsman redeemer (Lev. 25:23–24, 39–55). This law permitted a near relative to purchase back the property of a bankrupt Hebrew so that the land would not be lost from the family. In this situation the purchase would also include Ruth, the widow of Naomi's son Mahlon (Ruth 4:10).

It always encourages me when I read chapters 3 and 4 of Ruth, because what is recorded there reminds me of what Jesus has done for me. Boaz saw Ruth gleaning in the field, picking up the leftovers, and it was love at first sight. I was a lost sinner with nothing beautiful to admire in me, yet God in His love saw me and reached out to me. He providentially worked so that I might hear the good news of salvation, be convicted of my sin and trust Jesus as my Lord and Savior.

Chapter 3 informs us that Ruth had put herself at the feet of Boaz and declared her willingness to become his wife. In order to secure Ruth and the property, Boaz had to call a council meeting in the city gate and give a nearer kinsman first opportunity to make the purchase. But the man wouldn't make an offer because if he had Ruth as his wife, it would jeopardize his inheritance, so the way was opened for Boaz to act. (Jesus purchased us and *made us His inheritance!*) He paid the price and took Ruth out of the fields and into his heart and his home. She moved from poverty to riches, from loneliness to love, from weariness to rest, from being a stranger and nobody to becoming the wife of the lord of the harvest and the grandmother of David, Israel's greatest king. It was a miracle of the grace of God, and it all began when she clung to her mother-in-law and declared her faith in the true and living God.

Submission to God

When Ruth and Naomi left Moab, everything seemed against them. They were women heading for a nation that had a very masculine society. Ruth belonged to a pagan nation that was excluded from Israel by the very law of God. Ruth was a poor widow traveling with another poor widow, and widows didn't rank high in Israel. But her faith in the God of Israel had put hope in her heart. She submitted to Naomi and worked to care for her, and she submitted to Boaz and waited for him to act.

Suppose Ruth had gone back home as Orpah did?

Or, suppose she had sat at home and nursed a bitter spirit, as did Naomi at the beginning of their life in Bethlehem?

Or, suppose she had wandered into the wrong field and not been observed by Boaz?

Ruth permitted the Lord to have his way in her life, and she manifested that submissive spirit by caring for Naomi, working in the field, obeying the commands of Naomi and Boaz, and trusting the Lord to work out His will. After all, the will of God is the expression of the love of God for us, and His love never fails. "But the plans of the LORD stand firm forever, the purposes of his heart through all generations" (Ps. 33:11). God's will for us comes from God's heart, and our obedience must come from our hearts (Eph. 6:6).

The proof of God's love for us isn't found in the feelings within us or the circumstances around us. No matter how discouraging and difficult our circumstances may be, or how "low" we may feel, God still loves us and is working on our behalf (Rom. 8:28). How can we be sure? "But God demonstrates his own love for us in this: While we were still sinners, Christ died for us" (Rom. 5:8). He paid the purchase price to set us free from our old birth and give us a new birth that makes all things new! We know that God loves us because Jesus died for us.

Ruth trusted the Lord in everything and allowed Him to teach and direct her through ordinary people like Naomi, the field foreman, the harvesters and Boaz. The Lord used ordinary experiences like hunger and thirst, working and waiting, to accomplish His loving purposes. "If God is for us, who can be against us?" (Rom. 8:31). Day after day, she did in the strength of the Lord the ordinary things that other women were doing in Bethlehem, and she did them with gratitude to God. In the plan of God, there is no such thing as "secular" and "sacred," for "whether you eat or drink or whatever you do, do it all for the glory of God" (1 Cor. 10:31). If God has our everything, He can lead us in anything, especially the ordinary things we take for granted, like going off to work.

Each day, it has been my practice to commit my day and its schedule to the Lord, asking for His guidance and giving Him the right to make any changes that need to be made so His will is accomplished. I don't know how many times the interruptions have turned out to be the real ministries of the day and the disappointments have resulted in greater blessings than we had expected. G. Campbell Morgan used to say, "Disappointments—His appointments!"

"And now these three remain: faith, hope and love. But the greatest of these is love" (1 Cor. 13:13).

"His love endures forever." You find that statement twenty-six times in Psalm 136.

How many times must God say it before we will believe it and act accordingly?

7

David, the Appreciator

God is good, all the time!

What would a vocational guidance counselor do with a multi-gifted person like David?

He was a courageous shepherd who wasn't afraid to confront and kill a lion and a bear. Using only a stone and a sling, he also killed a giant whose size and words had paralyzed an entire army. David was an outstanding general whose wisdom and courage led his troops from victory to victory; yet at the same time he was a gifted poet and a musician whose psalms still inspire God's people. He handled a harp as well as he handled a sword. A compelling leader, he could formulate a battle plan or organize a building program, and all the while give glory to God. He was a remarkable man.

However, David also had his share of trials. He was the youngest in his family and his brothers didn't always understand him. (I sympathize with him: I was the "baby" in my family!) Though he was God's anointed king, for several years he had to hide in the wilderness lest King Saul's men should kill him. Saul's son Jonathan was

David's dearest friend, yet they were kept apart for years, and in the end Jonathan was killed on the battlefield. David passionately wanted to build a temple to honor the Lord, but God chose Solomon his son to do it instead. When you add to this list the many problems caused by enemy nations, the burdens of kingdom administration and the painful experiences in his own family, it's easy to see that David had his share of burdens as well as blessings.

But one aspect of David's personality is often overlooked: *he was a great appreciator.* David had a grateful heart and wasn't ashamed to express his gratitude to the Lord or to those who assisted him in his kingdom work. His many skills were all bound together by a heart that knew how to say, "Thank you!" In many of his psalms, he magnified the goodness of the Lord. "Taste and see that the LORD is good" (Ps. 34:8). "You, Lord, are forgiving and good, abounding in love for all who call to you" (Ps. 86:5). "Good and upright is the LORD; therefore he instructs sinners in his ways" (Ps. 25:8).

I believe that David's endurance during his many difficult times of trial was partly due to his thankful heart, an attitude of gratitude that kept him going no matter what obstacles he faced. He wrote in Psalm 27:13, "I remain confident of this: I will see the goodness of the LORD in the land of the living." When we get to heaven, God's people expect to discover how all things "worked together for good" during their time on earth (Rom. 8:28), but David expected to see God's goodness while he served on earth. That's faith! The New American Standard Bible translates Psalm 27:13, "I would have despaired unless I had believed that I would see the goodness of the LORD in the land of the living." God is good! All the time!

No matter where David looked, he saw the goodness of God, and this gave him strong faith in the greatness of God and His power to see him through. To David, the Lord was not a God far away but a Friend very near and very much involved in every facet of his life.

The Goodness of God

Whenever David looked up to the heavens, he thought of the goodness of the God above him. He knew that God was on the throne and that His goodness was great. Perhaps David remembered what Jehovah had said to Moses centuries before: "I will cause all my goodness to pass in front of you, and I will proclaim my name, the LORD, in your presence" (Exod. 33:19). The phrase "all my goodness" means "all my divine attributes," because every attribute of God is marked with His goodness.

Everything is good that He is, says and does, and it is all for our good, to accomplish His good purposes in this world. Even the painful experiences David encountered were good because they came from the heart of a good God. When God informed David that he would not build the temple, the king didn't complain or rebel. He simply said, "Sovereign LORD, you are God! Your covenant is trustworthy, and you have promised these good things to your servant" (2 Sam. 7:28). In Psalm 109:21 David writes about the goodness of God's love, and in Psalm 145:7 he speaks of God's "abundant goodness."

What David wrote in Psalm 31:19 should encourage us: "How great is your goodness, which you have stored

up for those who fear you." The Father in heaven loves us
so much that He has already stored up the good things
He knows we will need in the future. This means we can
walk calmly into each new day and be confident of God's
goodness as we do His will, for "no good thing does he
withhold from those whose walk is blameless" (Ps. 84:11).
"His divine power has given us everything we need for a
godly life through our knowledge of him who called us
by his own glory and goodness" (2 Pet. 1:3). He supplies
everything we need—and God's riches in Christ are
never affected by the stock market or the world economy
(Phil. 4:19).

During their thirty-eight years' march in the wilderness (Deut. 2:14), the Hebrew people received bread
from heaven six mornings a week. I think of that miracle
whenever I pray, "Give us today our daily bread" (Matt.
6:11). Even the wild creatures depend on their Creator
for their food. "All creatures look to you to give them their
food at the proper time. When . . . you open your hand,
they are satisfied with good things" (Ps. 104:27–28). It
all seems so simple: God knows the need, He opens His
hand and the need is met.

God's Goodness in Creation

This leads us logically to assume that when David
looked around, he saw the goodness of the Lord. David
was a sturdy outdoorsman who spent his youthful years
as a shepherd and his mature years as a soldier. During
his exile years, when he was hiding from Saul, David
made the wilderness of Judea his hiding place, and the

caves were his homes. When we read his psalms, it's no surprise that we see the world of nature and meet a man who paid attention to the useful and beautiful things that God had created.

David may have written Psalm 29 when he was stranded in a cave during a terrific thunder storm, and what a psalm it is! Not only can we see the storm and hear it, but we can almost feel it. David saw in that storm the strength and glory of God, and he called on the angels to worship the Lord as they watched the storm from their heavenly home. David said that the thunder was God's voice, powerful and majestic, shaking things and breaking things and making the mountains dance like calves freed from their stalls. "The LORD sits enthroned over the flood; the LORD is enthroned as King forever" (v. 10). As long as Jehovah was on the throne, David had no fear of the storm or of King Saul and his spies.

In Psalm 31 we don't hear a storm, but we see rocks and a cave. "In you, LORD, I have taken refuge; . . . be my rock of refuge, a strong fortress to save me" (vv. 1–2). As David communed with the Lord and prayed, God stood by David and transformed that dismal cave into a Holy of Holies. God gave David freedom from fear and adequate strength to keep going. Often in his psalms, David used the image of the rock as a reminder that God would protect him. "The LORD is my rock, my fortress and my deliverer; my God is my rock, in whom I take refuge" (Ps. 18:2). Read the entire psalm and note the images that make this psalm a picture gallery of God's grace and power. The message is clear: David saw the goodness of God in the world around him.

In the creation account in Genesis 1 and 2, each of the first five days ended with God examining His work and saying "Good!" On the sixth day, He examined the finished work and said "Very good!" In spite of the ravages of sin and human greed, there's no denying that creation is stamped with the goodness of God. Jesus saw the Father's providential care in creation and this was to Him the secret of an untroubled heart (Matt. 6:24– 34). The birds know that the Father will feed them, so they don't worry; and the flowers know the Father will clothe them with beauty, so they don't fret. I wonder if an ornithologist has ever found a robin suffering from stomach ulcers?

I'm writing these words on a sunny March morning. I took time to watch the birds at the feeders and to look at the flowers that are now bringing beauty to our yard. It did me good. "He makes grass to grow for the cattle, and plants for people to cultivate—bringing forth food from the earth" (Ps. 104:14). We can't live without food, though we could manage to live without beauty—yet the Lord gives us both! They shout to us, "Stop! Look! Listen! The Father is caring for us and for you! Calm down!" According to Jesus, the Father "causes his sun to rise on the evil and the good, and sends rain on the righteous and the unrighteousness" (Matt. 5:45). We all depend on God's goodness, whether we acknowledge it or not—but we should acknowledge it!

"Taste and see that the Lord is good; blessed are those who take refuge in him" (Ps. 34:8). No matter what our burdens may be, let's take time to look around at the Father's workmanship and praise Him for His goodness.

God's Future Goodness

Once our spiritual vision gets adjusted to see God's goodness above us and around us, we will become more like David and begin to anticipate God's goodness *before* us. In Psalm 21:1–2 David looked back and thanked God because He had strengthened him and answered his prayers. But in verse 3 David *looked ahead* and anticipated even more of God's blessing: "You came to greet him with rich blessings." I like that word "greet." "For you meet him with the blessings of goodness" (NKJV).

The Authorized Version reads, "For thou preventest him with the blessings of goodness." In the 17th century the word "prevent" meant "to come before, to anticipate, to precede." It also gives us our English word "providence," which means "to see to it beforehand." David is saying, "We don't know what lies ahead, but the Lord is already there and He will supply everything we need." One of the special names of the Lord is "Jehovah Jireh—the Lord will see to it" (Gen. 22:14).

In His sermon in John 10 about the Good Shepherd, Jesus said, "When he has brought out all his own, he goes ahead of them, and his sheep follow him because they know his voice" (v. 4). You can drive cattle, but you must lead sheep. If as obedient sheep we listen to His voice in the Word and obediently follow the Shepherd, we need never fear the future, for our Shepherd is already there with the blessings that we need. When David was a shepherd, he went before the sheep and carefully examined the pastures to make sure everything was safe, and in that way he "prepared a table before them" (Ps. 23:5). This is what the Lord does for us, if we follow Him.

For several years, I met with a dedicated young man who was preparing for ministry and had a problem trusting God for the unknown. He had a brilliant mind and was working on an engineering degree, but he wanted the Lord to supply a blueprint for each new step he had to take.

Of course, God doesn't give us detailed blueprints, because we can't grow in faith unless we walk by faith. He has given us what we need: His Word, the Holy Spirit, the counsel of His people *and the assurance of His providence.* "For this God is our God for ever and ever; he will be our guide even to the end" (Ps. 48:14). "And God is able to bless you abundantly, so that in all things at all times, having all that you need, you will abound in every good work" (2 Cor. 9:8).

I'm happy to say that today my friend is faithfully serving the Lord and doesn't seem to be searching for blueprints and timetables.

Paul's assurance to us is that "he who began a good work in you will carry it on to completion until the day of Christ Jesus" (Phil. 1:6). "For we are God's handiwork, created in Christ Jesus to do good works, which God prepared in advance for us to do" (Eph. 2:10). He works in us that He might work through us, and He has the blueprints.

During my years of ministry, it's been a joy to speak at various Keswick conferences, and I have especially enjoyed singing from the Keswick hymnals. Here are some stanzas from one of my favorites, written by Joseph Parker:

God holds the key of all unknown,
And I am glad;
If other hands should hold the key,
Or if He trusted it to me,
I might be sad.

. . . .

I cannot read His future plans;
But this I know:
I have the smiling of His face,
And all the refuge of His grace,
While here below.

Enough! This covers all my wants,
And so I rest!
For what I cannot, He can see,
And in His care I saved shall be,
Forever blest.

What should be our heart's response to the tremendous truth that God goes before us and prepares everything for our arrival? For one thing, trusting God's providence ought to keep us from fearing to obey Him and, when we do obey, stop us from worrying about the future. Faith in God's goodness should also encourage us to keep alert so we don't miss what is waiting for us at each place He directs us. We ought to be eagerly anticipating each day and looking for God's surprises, no matter where He leads us. Even more, let's cultivate grateful hearts and never cease to thank the Lord for His providential care. Satan wants us to believe that God is holding out on us (see Gen. 3:1–5), and the world that it has something better to offer us (1 John 2:15–17), but neither one is telling the truth. God always gives His best to those who leave the choice with Him.

God's Tapestry of Goodness

God's goodness is above us, safely stored to be dispensed as we need it. God's goodness is seen around us in the world God has made, and His goodness is waiting for us as we follow Jesus, the Good Shepherd, on the path of life. The future is our friend when Jesus is our Lord. But whenever our faith journey shall end, we shall look back and discover that God's goodness and unfailing love have followed us every day that we have lived (Ps. 23:6)! It may not look that way today, but when we reach the Father's house and look back, we will rejoice and say, "It has been *only* goodness and love!"

Then, let's believe that truth *now* and see the difference it will make in our lives!

One of the most fascinating metaphors for death was written by King Hezekiah after God had healed him of an illness that threatened his life. "Like a weaver I have rolled up my life, and he has cut me from the loom" (Isa. 38:12). Life is a weaving; death is being cut from the loom. Today as we make decisions, we weave the fabric of life, but we see only the underside and there doesn't seem to be much of a pattern. But one day we shall be "on the other side" and see the whole picture; and our hearts and lips will be filled with praise to the Lord, the Master Weaver!

My wife and I once visited a weaver's studio in the

hills of Kentucky, and when nobody was watching, I quickly looked under several looms. I saw no beauty; I saw only threads in disarray and colors in confusion. Yes, we make mistakes, we think nothing makes sense and we want to give up; but the Lord keeps weaving and always follows His perfect pattern. The time will come when we will see the complete pattern and fully understand the Lord's beautiful plan.

Meanwhile, let's rest on the assurance in Romans 8:28 and Psalm 23:6, knowing that God is *today* making all things work together for good and that His goodness and love are following us *today* and will follow us all the days that we live.

Hallelujah, what a Savior!

Like David, let's be true appreciators. God is good—all the time! And it's always too soon to quit.

8

Jeremiah, the "Traitor"

What God begins, He will complete.

Jeremiah's name is found in the English dictionary in the word *jeremiad*, which means "a prolonged lamentation, a mournful complaint." It's a reference to Jeremiah's tears and grief recorded in his prophecy and the Book of Lamentations. But Jeremiah had every reason to weep, for the leaders of the kingdom of Judah were persistently rebelling against the Lord, and the people were following their bad example. The nation had broken their covenant with God and were about to suffer the terrible consequences at the hands of Nebuchadnezzar and the Babylonian army, but very few were crying out to God for mercy.

For forty years Jeremiah preached the Word and pleaded with the people to repent and return to a sincere worship of the true and living God, but they refused to listen. Instead, they plunged deeper and deeper into idolatry, immorality and futile attempts to get help from everybody except the God of their fathers. Jeremiah told them to surrender to the Babylonians and the Lord would spare Jerusalem and the temple, but this counsel only made them call Jeremiah a traitor. During his ministry, he was arrested and imprisoned, beaten, put in the stocks and even dropped into a filthy cistern and left to die. When his messages from the Lord were read to King Jehoiakim, the king burned the scroll, section by section, and showed no fear of the Lord (Jer. 36).

But Jeremiah was not a traitor; he was a faithful citizen and a covenant-keeping Jew, and he alone had the remedy for the nation's plight. The real traitors were the priests and the false prophets (Jer. 6:13–15; 23:11–12; 26:7–11, 16), the king and his officers, and even Jeremiah's own family who had plotted to kill him (Jer. 12:5–6). Jeremiah was treated by his own people just as Jesus and the apostles were treated centuries later, and like them, he stayed true to the Lord and faithful to his ministry. His life was in danger, but he would not quit. The words of Paul to the believers in Philippi explain how Jeremiah kept going: "being confident of this, that he who began a good work in you will carry it on to completion ..." (Phil. 1:6). What the Lord starts, He finishes.

Sustained by God's Call

Perhaps the first and most important encouragement in the prophet's life and ministry was the assurance that God had called him. His call was not as spectacular as that of Isaiah, who saw the glorious throne of God in heaven (Isa. 6), or of Ezekiel, who saw God's throne carried by living creatures in the midst of a storm (Ezek. 1–3). Here is Jeremiah's simple account of his call:

The word of the LORD came to me, saying, "Before I formed you in the womb I knew you, before you were born I set you apart; I appointed you as a prophet to the nations. (Jer. 1:5)

The phrase "I knew you" means "I chose you," what the theologians call *divine election*. Jeremiah was chosen to be a prophet before he was even conceived in his mother's womb! He was born to be a priest, but God called him to the much more difficult ministry of a prophet. The work of the Levitical priest was somewhat routine and was spelled out in the Law of Moses; but the work of a prophet was usually unpredictable, and at times unsafe. God gave three anointed ministries to the Jewish people: king, priest and prophet; and when the kings and priests disobeyed God's law and led the people astray, the prophets had to call them back to faithfulness to the Lord and His Word. It wasn't an easy task. More than one prophet has been martyred.

Of course, God's call places on us an obligation to obey, whether we think we are qualified or not. Jeremiah thought he was too young to be a successful prophet, and not gifted enough to speak God's Word (1:6). But God made it clear that His call was more than an obligation; it was an opportunity to rescue the kingdom of Judah from ruin and for Jeremiah to grow spiritually while serving God and the people. Jeremiah served for over forty years, but the nation never did repent and return to the Lord. The false prophets preached a popular message of "peace and safety," and the people listened to them, but the people closed their ears to what Jeremiah had to say about sin and judgment.

Jeremiah had no band of disciples to assist him and no wife to encourage him. Zedekiah, the last king of Judah, feared his officials more than he feared the Lord, even though at the last minute he could have saved the city and the temple (Jer. 38:14–28). After the fall of the city, Jeremiah was forced to go to Egypt with a group of Jews, and there he died. From the human point of view, Jeremiah was a failure; but from God's point of view, he had fulfilled his calling and was a success.

I know from experience that there are times in the Lord's work when circumstances are painful and impossible to understand, when people are cruel and unbending, and when we wonder if the Lord hears our desperate prayers. It is in those times we must remind ourselves, "God called me here and gave me a work to complete, and therefore He will keep me here and see me through, if I keep His glory uppermost as I trust and obey. What God starts, He finishes."

God reminded Jeremiah that He made him what he was, set him apart, ordained him and would give him the messages for Judah and the other nations. He was equipped by the Lord and would be enabled by the Lord. Jeremiah was to be a distributor, not a manufacturer; whatever God commanded him to say, he proclaimed (1:7). The work would not be easy. Jeremiah would have to root up before he could plant, and tear down before he could build (1:10). The nation was at the crossroads, so the prophet had to stand there and point the people in the right direction (6:16). He was to be a physician and probe deeply into their hearts (6:14; 8:11, 22), as well as an assayer who wasn't afraid to turn up the heat and test the quality of the metal (6:27–30).

Jeremiah knew that God had called him and therefore would see him through.

Sustained by God's Word

Jeremiah was sustained by his calling from God and also by the word that God gave him. A prophet without a word from the Lord is not really a prophet at all. As you read the Book of Jeremiah, you frequently find statements like "The Lord said to me" and "The word of the Lord came to me saying" and "Hear the word of the Lord." The Hebrew word translated *hear*, *listen* and *obey* is used nearly two hundred times in his book. Jeremiah didn't want a surface ministry that tickled people's ears; he wanted the Word to penetrate their hearts and transform their lives.

Early in Jeremiah's ministry, godly King Josiah had led the people in a national reformation that cleansed the idols out of the land, but wasn't thorough enough to change the people's hearts. After Josiah died the people quickly reverted to their former evil ways. The word "heart" is found some seventy times in Jeremiah's prophecy. He knew that the human heart was sick from sin and that the Lord examined hearts and knew every secret (17:9–10). A lasting ministry of depth is a ministry of the Word, from God's heart to the hearts of needy people, through the loving and burdened heart of the preacher, teacher or witness.

When we fail to proclaim the Word of God, we grieve the Holy Spirit who wrote it, and we also grieve Jesus about whom the Scriptures were written. God doesn't listen to our clever ideas and try to decide how to use them. He watches over His Word and sees to it that it does its job (1:12; see also Isa. 55:11). Jeremiah rejoiced in God's Word and was nourished by it (15:16), for if we don't feed ourselves, how can we feed others? If a Bible class is only fun and games, and a sermon is only an ethical essay, how can sinners be saved and believers built up? We are living in the days that Amos wrote about, days of a famine of God's Word (Amos 9:11). Exposition has been replaced by entertainment, and the saints languish.

As I review the years of our ministry, I recall those special times when God pointed us to the Word because it had the answer to our questions or the assurances for our fears. My wife and I don't play "Bible roulette" and open the Bible just anywhere and point to a verse, but we listen for God's voice in the course of our individual daily devotions as well as our devotional times together each morning. We can testify that the Lord has always given us direction from the Scriptures, no matter what decisions, trials or changes we might be facing. Joshua said it best: "You know with all your heart and soul that not one of all the good promises the LORD your God gave you has failed" (Josh. 23:14).

Sustained by Prayer

Jeremiah listened when the Lord spoke to him, and the Lord listened when Jeremiah spoke to Him in his prayers.[1] Like the early apostles, the prophet devoted his attention "to prayer and the ministry of the word" (Acts 6:4), and so should we today. We can "manufacture results" without praying, but we cannot bear lasting fruit that glorifies God. Without prayer we can build a crowd, but not a Spirit-led church, and we can give religious speeches, but not life-changing sermons that expound God's truth. Because the kingdom of Judah was under God's judgment, three times God told Jeremiah to stop interceding for them (7:16; 11:14; 14:11); but He never told His servant to stop praying. Prayer helped to keep Jeremiah going when it seemed like everything was against him.

No sooner did the Lord call Jeremiah into His service than the young man prayed! "Ah, Sovereign LORD, I do not know how to speak; I am too young" (Jer. 1:6). The answer came immediately, for the Lord told him to go where he was sent, to speak the words he was given, and not to be afraid. When God revealed that judgment was coming to Judah from the north, Jeremiah asked why the other prophets were preaching a message of peace and safety (4:5–10). He asked for wisdom to understand what was happening (James 1:5), and the Lord told him what he needed to know. In 9:1–3, he prayed for a greater ability to weep over the people, but he also asked for a safe place in the wilderness where he could "get away from it all" and have some peace. Can you blame him? David prayed a similar prayer in Psalm 55:6–8. In 10:23–25 Jeremiah asked God to discipline the nation for disobeying His law. "Remember me and care for me!" he prayed in 15:15–18, and he called God his "strength and fortress" in 16:19–20.

I recommend that you meditate on Jeremiah's prayers and see how they relate to what Jesus taught us about prayer. In the Book of Lamentations, the prayers are in 1:20–22, 2:20–22, 3:52–66 and 5:1–22. If at times

Jeremiah seems impatient with both the Lord and the people of Judah, keep in mind that he was human like the rest of us and often endured great humiliation and pain. "Since my people are crushed, I am crushed; I mourn, and horror grips me" (Jer. 8:21). Should you ever feel like that, take it to the Lord in prayer.

Understanding the Times

The prophet knew his times—the way the people lived, the leaders they followed and the lies they believed. He also recognized that the people and their leaders were spiritually blind and deaf, and willfully ignorant of God's truth. The priests should have been pointing the people to the Word of God; instead, they sided with the political leaders and led the people astray. The false prophets were especially popular because they proclaimed an easy message based on a false hope. "They dress the wound of my people as though it were not serious. 'Peace, peace,' they say, when there is no peace" (Jer. 6:14). "Both prophet and priest are godless," said the Lord through His faithful servant; "even in my temple I find their wickedness" (23:11).

The humiliating defeat of Judah and the terrible destruction of the city and the temple could be blamed on the false prophets, the compromising priests and the vacillating policies of a series of weak kings and their flattering officers. The false prophets made it easy for the priests and the political leaders to spread their lies and build false hopes. "Do not listen to what the prophets are prophesying to you," the Lord said; "they fill you with false hopes. They speak visions from their own minds, not from the mouth of the LORD ... they say, 'No harm will come to you'" (23:16–17). However, harm did come! "But it happened because of the sins of her prophets and the iniquities of her priests" (Lam. 4:13).

Among the warriors who joined David during his exile were men from the tribe of Issachar "who understood the times and knew what Israel should do" (1 Chron. 12:32). Certainly it's necessary for an army to have men who are skillful with weapons and brave in heart, but it's also necessary to have soldiers who know the meaning of events and what God's people should do. Jeremiah wasn't in the army, but he understood the times and the mistakes the leaders were making, *but they would not listen to him!*

The Lord said through His servant,

> Let not the wise boast of their wisdom, or the strong boast of their strength, or the rich boast of their riches, but let those who boast boast about this: that they understand and know me, that I am the LORD, who exercises kindness, justice and righteousness on earth, for in these I delight. (Jer. 9:23–24)

The kingdom of Judah was depending on the assets that nations have always trusted: human wisdom, human strength and human wealth. But when the Babylonian army surrounded Jerusalem, none of these so-called assets could rescue the city, the temple or the people. These assets became liabilities because they kept the people from trusting in the Lord.

Jeremiah understood this truth and devoted himself to warning the leaders and the people to return to the Lord, but they didn't understand the times because they wanted their own way. They chose the "easiest way," but it turned out to be the hardest way.

Churches and individual believers today make the same mistake when they put their trust in anything but the Lord. The church at Corinth, for example, was proud of its wealth, wisdom and demonstrations of spiritual power, but Paul reminded them that their assets were only liabilities if they failed to submit to the Lord and trust Him, and he even quoted from Jeremiah (1 Cor. 1:18–30; 2 Cor. 10:12–18). God isn't impressed with our real estate, budgets, crowds or press releases. If people leave a service impressed by the preacher, awed by the music, or overwhelmed by the architecture instead of glorying in the Lord, then the service was a failure.

If we are to serve the Lord effectively, we must avoid following popular illusions and see things as they truly are. Both Jeremiah and Jesus wept over Jerusalem, because they could read the signs of the times and understand the divine plan.

Understanding Our Weaknesses

Centuries before Paul wrote Second Corinthians 12:1–10, Jeremiah knew the basic truth the apostle wrote about: "for when I am weak, then I am strong" (v. 10). In the Christian life, weakness that knows itself to be weakness can become strength, but strength that knows itself to be strength will eventually become weakness. Uzziah, one of Judah's greatest kings, become proud and attempted to enter the holy precincts of the temple, and God smote him with leprosy. "But after Uzziah became powerful, his pride led to his downfall" (2 Chron. 26:16). Jeremiah knew he was weak, but he also knew that God would strengthen him for his ministry. Jeremiah was strong before men but weak before God, and that's why he didn't quit.

"Since my people are crushed," said the prophet, "I am crushed; I mourn and horror grips me. . . . Oh, that my head were a spring of water and my eyes a fountain of tears! I would weep day and night for the slain of my people" (8:21; 9:1). When Jeremiah wanted to debate with the Lord about the seeming injustice of events (5:1–4), God's answer was, "If you have raced with people on foot and they have worn you out, how can you compete with horses? If you stumble in safe country, how will you manage in the thickets by the Jordan?" (12:5). In other words, "Your work will become more difficult and demanding, but the challenge will build and strengthen you. I want to give you the strength of a horse and the courage to face the lions in the jungles of the Jordan. Your circumstances will get more difficult, but you will grow stronger."

Quitters use their weaknesses as an excuse for dropping out of the running, but winners fix their eyes on Jesus and run the race with endurance (Heb. 12:1–3). During months of therapy after shoulder surgery, I discovered that the therapy had to hurt if it was going to bring about healing. My excellent therapist knew exactly how much to "challenge" my shoulder, and eventually my weakness became strength. Each visit introduced me to new demands that helped me develop new strength, so the pain was worth it.

They tell me it's a mark of maturity when we recognize our weaknesses, accept them and cooperate with the

Lord in turning them into strengths. Many of the people found in the Scriptures failed in their strengths, not their weaknesses. Abraham was a man of great faith, and that's where he failed because he ran to Egypt for help. Moses was a meek man, yet he sinned and was disciplined because he lost his temper (Num. 20). Solomon was a man of great wisdom, but he listened to his pagan wives and worshiped idols. Peter was a courageous man, yet he wilted before a servant girl and denied his Lord.

Achievers are believers. By faith they obey God in spite of their sense of weakness, and God turns that weakness into strength.

Understanding that God Is With Us

"Do not be afraid of them, for I am with you and will rescue you," the Lord promised the young prophet (Jer. 1:8), and then repeated the promise in verse 19: "They will fight against you but will not overcome you, for I am with you and will rescue you" (see also Jer. 15:20; 42:11; 46:28). That was the Lord's promise to Jeremiah, and it is His promise to His children today. "Never will I leave you; never will I forsake you" (Deut. 31:6; Heb. 13:5). "And surely I am with you always, to the very end of the age" (Matt. 28:20). "I am with you . . . to the very end!" Not just the end of the age but also to the very end of each assignment, each responsibility, each battle, each appointment, each trial—yes, even to the end of each life!

Early in his second letter to Timothy, Paul wrote, "You know that everyone in the province of Asia has deserted me" (2 Tim.1:15). Near the close of his letter, he wrote, "At my first defense, no one came to my support, but everyone deserted me. . . . But the Lord stood at my side and gave me strength, so that through me the message might be fully proclaimed and all the Gentiles might hear it. And I was delivered from the lion's mouth" (2 Tim. 4:16–17). Paul was deserted by the very people he had led to Christ, but the Christ who had saved Paul did not desert him. At his conversion Paul heard Jesus say, "I will rescue you from your own people and from the Gentiles" (Acts 26:15–18), and Jesus kept that promise. He is Immanuel—God with us (Matt. 1:22–23).

It made no difference to Jeremiah who sat on the throne of Judah, because he got his orders from the Lord enthroned in heaven, the Lord who promised always to be with him. The throne of David had been defiled and its last king (Zedekiah) would be blinded and bound and taken to Babylon. The throne of God in the temple (the ark, Ps. 80:1) would have no resting place because the temple would be destroyed. But God's throne would endure forever! Jeremiah sang, "A glorious throne, exalted from the beginning, is the place of our sanctuary" (Jer. 17:12). When the servants of God are doing the will of God and trusting the promises of God, they may always be certain of the presence of God to help them accomplish the will of God.

Before he died John Wesley cried out twice, "Best of all, God is with us!" And then he said, "Farewell."

Standing for Truth

As we follow Jesus day by day, our lives will become more and more counter-cultural, and this means we will be treated like traitors as was Jeremiah. "They will put you out of the synagogue," Jesus told His disciples; "in fact the hour is coming when those who kill you will think they are offering a service to God. They will do such things because they have not known the Father or me" (John 16:2–3). He said, "Blessed are those who are persecuted because of righteousness, for theirs is the kingdom of heaven" (Matt. 5:10).

The world by and large doesn't want truth, because truth forces people to think and make decisions, and people don't like to do that. Knowing truth might even make them uncomfortable. But Jesus *is* the truth (John 14:6), and unbelievers don't want Jesus *or anybody who acknowledges Jesus as Savior and Lord*. It's a battle between truth and lies, and I'm reminded of the statement attributed to Mark Twain: "A lie can travel halfway around the world while the truth is putting on its shoes." Something within the heart of humans enjoys believing lies, and that something is what the Bible calls sin. "The heart is deceitful above all things and beyond cure, who can understand it?" The "treacherous" prophet Jeremiah said that (Jer. 17:9).

But our counter-cultural crowd is in good company. The apostles got in trouble because they said Jesus was alive and that the temple would be destroyed, and Paul was accused of preaching another king than Caesar, a man called Jesus (Acts 17:1–9). The world says Jesus is just another dead teacher, but Christian believers say He is alive, reigning in heaven, and will come again. The world says the Bible is only another religious book, but believers say it is the inspired Word of God. The world says that one religion is as good as another, because all religious roads lead to heaven; but Christians affirm that there is only one way to heaven, and that way is repentance for sin and faith in Jesus Christ, the Son of God.

In short, from the world's viewpoint, Christian believers are counter-cultural and perhaps even slightly deranged, and therefore, they are traitors. Well, our Lord's family said of Jesus, "He is out of his mind" (Mark 3:20–21), and the Roman governor Festus shouted at Paul, "You are out of your mind, Paul! Your great learning is driving you insane!" (Acts 26:24).

What God begins, He will complete.

Have you made that new beginning with Jesus and been born again?

9

Habakkuk, the Wrestler

Face the facts, but keep living by faith.

The name *Habakkuk* means "to wrestle, to embrace." More about that later.

It's generally agreed among students of the Old Testament that Habakkuk and Jeremiah were contemporaries in Jerusalem when the kingdom of Judah was falling apart. The nation was in political decline and spiritual decay, thanks to the stupidity and disobedience of a series of kings who refused to obey God's Word. Their rebellion against the Lord meant that God would have to keep the terms of the covenant He made with His people and chasten them for their sins (Deut. 28:45–52; 2 Chron. 36:11–19). It also meant that the Babylonians would invade Judah, destroy Jerusalem and the temple, and deport thousands of Jews to Babylon.

We know a great deal about Jeremiah and his ministry, and practically nothing about the man Habakkuk and the work he did. Jeremiah experienced a lifetime of burdens and battles as he pleaded with the people to return to God, while Habakkuk seems to have had one major personal conflict with God from which he emerged a smarter and a better man. That conflict is recorded in the Book of Habakkuk, a book that is brief but profound. Jeremiah had to fight external battles that even threatened his life, but Habakkuk faced problems in his heart and mind as he tried to understand what God was doing to His people. It's difficult to live by faith and serve the Lord when your theology says one thing and your Master seems to be doing something else.

Here's a brief outline of the prophet's "wrestling match" with Jehovah.

1. Habakkuk withstands God and is brought low as he questions God (chap. 1)
   a. Why don't you do something? (1:1–4); God's reply (1:5–11)
   b. Why use wicked Babylon to punish your chosen people? (1:12–17)

2. Habakkuk stands before God and goes higher as he listens to God (chap. 2)
   a. God points out Judah's many sins
   b. God states three basic principles for spiritual victory
      • God blesses faith and faithfulness (2:4)
      • God will ultimately receive glory (2:14)
      • God's sovereign rule will prevail (2:20)

3. Habakkuk understands God and praises God in the heights (chap. 3)
   a. Renewing (3:1–2)
   b. Remembering (3:3–15)

c. Resolving (3:16)
d. Rejoicing (3:17–19)

It's clear that Habakkuk had a dramatic change of *attitude* as well as a change of *altitude* as he moved from the depths of perplexity to the heights of praise. "The Sovereign LORD is my strength; he makes my feet like the feet of a deer, he enables me to tread on the heights" (3:19). He began in what John Bunyan's *Pilgrim's Progress* called "the slough of despond," then moved to the top of his watchtower, and finally he reached the peaks of the mountains, bounding like a deer. He went from worrying to worshiping, because he took time to be quiet and listen to God.

At Least He Was Honest

Let's give Habakkuk credit for his transparency as he cried out to God for help. It's true that the prophet's attitude was somewhat imperious as he demanded that the Lord explain what He was doing. Habakkuk had been faithfully praying and even crying out to God, and had received no answer (1:1–2), so he began to ask questions as though God owed him an explanation for His actions. Job made a similar mistake, you may recall.

Habakkuk asked the Lord two questions: "How long must I pray before you answer?" and "Why do you permit such injustice?" There is nothing wrong with humbly asking God to teach us, but we must be careful not to issue orders. Even Jesus asked, "How long . . . ?" (Matt. 17:17) and "Why . . . ?" (Matt. 27:45–46), and the Father didn't rebuke Him.

Habakkuk's first problem was the seeming indifference of God to the plight of His people: "Why aren't you doing something about the mess the nation is in?" The prophet had received no answer to his prayers, and it seemed to him that the Lord was indifferent to Judah's dangers. Josiah's reform hadn't really changed things, the priests and prophets were liars and extortionists, and the nation desperately needed to repent and turn to God. Habakkuk uses words like strife, violence, iniquity, injustice and wrongdoing to describe the society of his day. The law was paralyzed and the judges were selling themselves to the highest bidders.

The Lord's answer shocked the prophet: "I *am* at work! What I'm doing is so remarkable that you won't believe it. I'm permitting the idolatrous Babylonians to invade Judah, destroy the city and the temple, and take the people captive." This was an answer the prophet didn't want to hear, and it only raised a second question: "How can you punish your own people by bringing against them a people more wicked than they are? Israel is your covenant people and you treat us this way? You should be roaring against the enemy, and yet heaven is silent. Why punish Judah when you ought to be punishing Babylon?"

Habakkuk knew his theology (1:12–13). God is eternal and therefore sovereign, and God is holy and therefore sinless; in fact, He is so holy that He cannot tolerate sin. He knows how the enemy will treat His people and yet He says nothing and does nothing! The people of Judah were helpless but God sent them no help. It was true that the Babylonians were a ruthless, vicious people and that their sins were many and great; *but the sins of God's people were far worse than the sins of a pagan nation.* God's judgment begins with the household of the Lord (1 Pet. 4:17; see also Ezek. 9:6). The Jewish people were God's chosen people, and their election involved responsibility. "You only have I chosen of all the families of the earth; therefore I will punish you for all your sins" (Amos 3:2). To whom much is given, much is required, and privilege involves responsibility.

On his first missionary journey, Paul met a group of Jewish people who opposed his preaching of the gospel, and Paul quoted Habakkuk 1:5 to them: "For I am going to do something in your days that you would not believe, even if I told you" (see Acts 13:38–41). In Habakkuk's day God used the Gentiles to bring punishment to the disobedient Jews; but in Paul's day God used the Jews to bring the salvation message to the Gentiles! If the Jews rejected the truth, the Gentiles would accept it. Babylon destroyed Jerusalem in Habakkuk's day, and Rome would destroy Jerusalem in 70 AD. God's ways are certainly above our ways.

A Time for Silence

There is "a time to be silent and a time to speak" (Eccl. 3:7), and the time had come for Habakkuk to be silent so God could speak to him again. In the average worship service, if the leader calls for a time of silent meditation and prayer, most of the saints become impatient and fidgety. Instead of watching and praying, they are looking at their watches and not praying. We live in a noisy society, and many people depend on voices or music to distract them from themselves and their problems. They don't like silence. To them, silence isn't golden—it's poison. They can't maintain a few minutes of silence in church because they haven't had much practice being silent before God elsewhere and meditating on His Word.

Habakkuk saw himself as a watchman on the city walls, scanning the landscape for the approaching enemy armies. Isaiah had used the same image (Isa. 21:6–16) and so had Habakkuk's fellow prophet Jeremiah (Jer. 6:16–19), and Ezekiel would be commissioned a watchman in Babylon (Ezek. 3:17–21; 33:1–9). Prophets were seers as well as speakers, and as we read their messages, we must ask God to open the eyes of our hearts to see His truth afresh (Eph. 1:17). Habakkuk the wrestler had been struggling with the Lord, and now it was time for him to wait before the Lord and learn some of His secrets. This is a good example for us to follow.

But the message God shared wasn't only for the prophet; it was for everybody, including God's church today. The prophet was told to write the message large and clear on a tablet so that anybody who saw it could read it easily and then run and deliver God's Word to others. Judgment was coming and there was no time for delay. The leaders and the people of Judah were also sinners who needed to repent and begin once again to obey the Word of the Lord. God has His timetable for the nations, and our job is to obey Him, not advise Him.

It has well been said that the heart of every problem is the problem in the heart, whether the problem be personal, national or international. In chapter one Habakkuk had described the evil deeds of the Babylonians, but now the Lord will announce the sins of the Babylonians as well as the citizens of Judah. The first sin on the list is *pride*: they are "puffed up . . . arrogant and never at rest" (vv. 4–5). Babylon was indeed a vast and powerful empire, but only because the will of God permitted it. Nebuchadnezzar's boast reflects the pride of every arrogant achiever: "Is not this great Babylon I have built as the royal residence, by my mighty power and for the glory of my majesty?" (Dan. 4:30). No sooner had he spoken those words when the king became like a beast, and for seven years he ate grass like a beast and even looked like a beast. God didn't only humble the king; he humiliated him. But Zedekiah, king of Judah, would also be humiliated and his sons and officers slain.

Nebuchadnezzar needed to learn what many leaders have never learned, that the Most High God is sovereign over all the nations of the world (Dan. 4:32). Kings and queens, generals and presidents, and even governors and mayors, are all second in command. It's interesting that the Lord connects pride with wine, because even today we speak about people who are "drunk with pride." The Lord also connected pride with greed (v. 5), because proud people always want more and more wealth, power and territory, and they will go to any lengths to secure what they want. In contrast to the "puffed up" boasters are the humble believers: "but the righteous will live by their faithfulness" (v. 4). This statement is quoted in the New Testament as "the righteous shall live by faith" (Rom. 1:17; Gal. 3:11; Heb. 10:38). Since it requires faith to be faithful, there is no problem with the way the Holy Spirit used this verse in the New Testament. We will discuss this important verse later.

Judgment on Gentiles—and Jews

It must have encouraged Habakkuk to hear the Lord pronounce five woes upon the Babylonians (2:6–19), but surely he knew that these judgments also applied to the people of Judah (see Isa. 5.) Babylon's selfish ambition and abuse of power would bring sorrow and death to many people, but they would reap what they had sown. Jeremiah predicted the destruction of Babylon (Jer. 50–51), and so did Daniel when he interpreted the handwriting on the wall (Dan. 5). However, Zedekiah and his officers had permitted wealthy and influential people in Judah to abuse, exploit and even kill innocent people, so why should Judah escape punishment? God would judge the leaders in Judah who murdered people so they could plunder their wealth (vv. 6–8) and steal their land (vv. 9–11). In this way they built their cities "with bloodshed" (vv. 12–13), just as the Babylonians had done as they swept across the ancient Near East.

The Lord mentioned the sins of drunkenness, indecency and violence (vv. 15–17), and he closed with an indictment against those who worshiped idols (vv. 18–19). The city of Babylon was filled with idols, but Judah also had its share. God gave Ezekiel in Babylon a vision of idols in the very temple in Jerusalem (Ezek. 8–9), making it clear that what the elders were doing was wicked and detestable. If Habakkuk wanted the Lord to judge the evil Babylonians, could he explain why the leaders and people of Judah should escape *when they were committing the same sins and knew better?* Judgment begins with God's people, and the righteous Lord would deal with the thieves, murderers, crooked politicians, drunks and idol worshipers.

But there was hope. One of Habakkuk's prayers was "in wrath, remember mercy" (3:2), and the Lord would answer that prayer. In this message of judgment in chapter 2, the Lord graciously inserted three marvelous statements that are like beacon lights on a dark, stormy night: " . . . but the righteous will live by their faithfulness" (v. 4); "For the earth will be filled with the knowledge of the glory of the LORD as the waters cover the sea" (v. 14); "The LORD is in his holy temple; let all the earth be silent before him" (v. 20).

Righteousness by Faith

As mentioned before, Habakkuk 2:4—"the righteous will live by their faithfulness" (2:4)—is quoted three times in the New Testament as "The righteous [or my righteous one] will live by faith" (Rom. 1:17; Gal. 3:11; Heb. 10:38). There can be no faithfulness without faith, for true faith imparts God's life within us and this leads to righteous living (Rom. 5:18). "Justification" is the gracious act of God whereby He declares the believing sinner righteous in Christ. It is not a process but a crisis. It gives us a right standing before God that produces right living before others. It is not just a legal transaction, something recorded on the books of heaven. It is a personal matter, because the result of receiving God's free gift is "justification of life" (Rom. 5:18, NKJV).

It's remarkable that these seven simple words in the small book of Habakkuk required three books in the

New Testament for their explanation and application. Paul's letter to the Romans explains who "the just" are; the Galatian epistle describes how they should live; and the Book of Hebrews defines "by faith." Habakkuk 2:4 is certainly a key verse in Scripture.

"Puffed up" unbelievers have faith in themselves and want nothing to do with faith in Jesus Christ. They feel quite adequate when it comes to pleasing God and having the assurance of going to heaven. "God, I thank you that I am not like other people—robbers, evil doers, adulterers—or even like this tax collector. I fast twice a week and give a tenth of all I get" (Luke 18:11–12). However, it was the tax collector, not the Pharisee, who went home "justified before God" (Luke 18:14); for "God opposes the proud but shows favor to the humble and oppressed" (1 Pet. 5:5).

The just are not only saved by faith but they "live by faith, not by sight" (2 Cor. 5:7). It is by faith that we have access to God and can pray (Rom. 5:2; Eph. 3:12), and it is by faith that we encourage one another (Rom. 1:12). We stand firm by faith (2 Cor. 1:24) and understand and accomplish God's will by faith (Heb. 11). The Bible is "the word of faith" (Rom. 10:8), and our faith grows as we receive the Word of God (Rom. 10:17). Our victory over the world is through faith (1 John 5:4). Whatever we accomplish by faith brings glory to God, because it seems impossible that we could do it. Review Hebrews 11 and see what God did through ordinary people because they lived by faith. "If you do not stand firm in your faith, you will not stand at all" (Isa. 7:9).

The British preacher Geoffrey Studdert Kennedy used

to say that faith is not believing in spite of evidence—
that's superstition—but obeying in spite of consequence.
To obey God's will in spite of the feelings within us, the
circumstances around us or the consequences before us is
to live by faith. Read Hebrews 11 with that definition in
mind, and you will see how right Kennedy was. A friend,
now in heaven, had a 3 x 5 card under the glass on his
desk, on which he had written: "Faith is living without
scheming." Remembering that statement has helped me
many times.

Questioners like Habakkuk can become stronger
believers if they live by faith and humbly allow God to
know some things they don't know (Deut. 29:29). But
when questioners become doubters, they are in danger of
becoming outright unbelievers, and that leads to becoming
quitters. "But knowledge puffs up while love builds up" (1
Cor. 8:1). Even when we don't fully understand God's
thoughts or ways, we know we can trust His loving heart.

In verse 14 you find a second statement from the
Lord that encouraged Habakkuk: "For the earth will
be filled with the knowledge of the glory of the LORD
as the waters cover the sea." The kingdom of Judah was
about to be overrun by Babylonian soldiers who would
leave behind ruin and rubble, corpses and captives, and
a humiliated nation. At one time the glory of the Lord
had dwelt in the temple in Jerusalem (1 Kings 8:10), but
that would end. Ezekiel in Babylon saw in a vision the
glory depart from the temple because the leaders had
filled it with idols (Ezek. 8–11). "Ichabod, the glory has
departed from Israel" (1 Sam. 4:21–22). But the day will
come when God's glory will return to a new temple in

a new Jerusalem, and the glory of the Lord will radiate throughout the world (Ezek. 43:1–5).

God's glory cloud had led Israel from Egypt to the border of Canaan where Israel refused to trust God and enter the land. The Lord had to judge them for their unbelief, and the glory of God did not enter the Promised Land for thirty-eight years. But the Lord promised Moses, "Indeed, as I live, all the earth will be filled with the glory of the Lord" (Num. 14:21, NASB). Not just Canaan but all the earth! Our prayer should be, "Praise be to his glorious name forever; may the whole earth be filled with his glory" (Ps. 72:19).

When God looks down on our world, He sees wickedness, rebellion and corruption (Gen. 6:5; Ps. 2:1–3; 14:1–7), but that isn't the end of the story. The seraphs at the throne look down and see things from God's viewpoint, and they say, "Holy, holy, holy is the Lord Almighty; the whole earth is full of his glory" (Isa. 6:3). The world of nature still has beauty, but the world of humanity is a disappointment. However, God's angels see what the Lord is doing on this planet and *rejoice at the glory that comes to His name!* Read the newspapers or watch the television news and you will feel like giving up in unbelief, but listen to the report from God's throne— "the whole earth is full of his glory"—and your faith will be strengthened and you will not think of quitting. We pray "Your kingdom come," and one day God's glorious kingdom will fill the earth.

My wife is the gardener in our family. All winter she will nurture ugly bulbs in our storage room, but when spring arrives, she pots them and brings them upstairs to enjoy the sunlight coming through the picture window. New life quietly surges through the stems and leaves and before long we have gorgeous amaryllis plants! An ugly bulb becomes a beautiful flower because God the Creator built that miracle into the bulb. So it is with God's promises: what He promises will be fulfilled. You and I have the privilege of glorifying God today by the lives that we live and the work that we do. "Let your light so shine before men, that they may see your good works and glorify your Father in heaven" (Matt. 5:16).

God Is in Control

Habakkuk 2:4 reminds us to pay attention to God's promises, for *faith* and *promises* go together. The second statement (v. 14) points to God's glorious character and our responsibility to glorify Him on earth. But Habakkuk 2:20 exalts God's sovereign rule in this world: "The Lord is in his holy temple; let all the earth be silent before him." When through Jesus Christ we enter into God's presence, it's not so we can give Him advice but to ask Him for the wisdom and strength we need to serve Him each day. No matter who is in Congress or Parliament, no matter who is in the White House or the United Nations, *God is on the throne and He knows what He is doing!* No matter what happened to the temple in Jerusalem, the temple in heaven was safe and secure and God was in control.

I like that phrase "all the earth." Human governments are limited by authority and geography, but our God is in complete control of everything. Abraham called Him "the Judge of all the earth" (Gen. 18:25); Joshua said He is "the Lord of all the earth" (Josh. 3:11); the psalmist called

Him "the great King over all the earth" (Ps. 47:2). This doesn't mean that the Lord is to be blamed for everything that has happened or is happening in our world; but it does mean that where He is not permitted to rule, the Lord will overrule and accomplish His righteous purposes on all the earth. The sovereignty of God doesn't violate either human responsibility or personal accountability, but it does guarantee that when we pray "your kingdom come, your will be done, on earth as it is in heaven" (Matt. 6:10), we are not wasting our breath.

People who ought to know better think that the sovereignty of God puts us in jail wearing strait jackets, but just the opposite is true: God's sovereignty frees us to serve Him, to enjoy doing His will and to receive His blessings. At a particularly difficult time in my pastoral ministry, I felt like I was drowning in difficulties and impossible demands, when the Lord showed me Psalm 33:11: "But the plans of the Lord stand firm forever, the purposes of His heart through all generations." *God's sovereign will comes from God's loving heart and is an expression of His personal love for us!* What an encouraging revelation! It doesn't sound like sitting in jail, wearing a strait jacket!

Most of what goes on in our world is beyond our personal control. I can't control the weather, but with God's help I can respond to it in a mature manner and make the most of the situation. Other than praying, I can do little personally about the assassinations of leaders, the tyranny of dictators or the delays and cancellations of airplanes, but I can receive God's grace and act like a Christian. After all, I belong to the family of "God, the blessed and only Ruler, the King of kings and Lord of lords" (1 Tim. 6:15). If I really believe that, I will act accordingly. Beholding with a broken heart the ruins of Jerusalem, the prophet Jeremiah said it beautifully: "Who can speak and have it happen if the Lord has not decreed it? Is it not from the mouth of the Most High that both calamities and good things come?" (Lam. 3:37–38).

When our hearts are upset and our plans have been shattered, it isn't easy to be silent; but Habakkuk 2:20 instructs us to do just that: "be silent before him." This means no debating, no resisting, no bargaining, just silently submitting. "I put my hands over my mouth," Job said to the Lord. "I spoke once, but I have no answer— twice, but I will say no more" (Job. 40:5).

What a privilege it is to bow silently before the Lord, beholding His glory and waiting for the "gentle whisper" of His voice that follows the wind, the earthquake and the fire, *if* we wait long enough in silence. Solitude and silence are missing disciplines in Christian living today, because we want our lives to be noisy and crowded. "The purpose of silence and solitude is to be able to see and hear," wrote Richard Foster, but many Christians would rather be disturbed and distracted. They don't want to see and hear too much from the Lord; it might obligate them to have to do something.

A Prayer for Revival

The prophet reaches his highest spiritual elevation in chapter 3, for he ends up treading on the heights of the mountains in the strength of the LORD (v. 19). This chapter is called "a prayer of Habakkuk," but the phrase "on shigionoth" suggests it was intended for liturgical use in the temple. In the Hebrew text you will find a "selah" after the word "arrows" in v. 9 and also at the end of v. 13, which also suggests public worship. The chapter records the prophet's responses to what God had said to him and revealed to him (v. 16).

His prayer in verse 2 begins with a request that God renew the mighty deeds He had performed for His people in the past, deeds described in verses 3 through 15. He had already asked God why He was doing nothing, and God had told him He was already at work (1:2–4); so Habakkuk prayed that the Lord would revive His work, make it known and keep it going. The prophet realized that the Babylonian attack on Judah was also part of that work, and he prayed God would show mercy to Judah even as He permitted the nation to be chastened.

Before we pray about present needs or impending challenges, it helps to increase our faith if we remember the mighty works of God in the past. The prophet does this in verses 3 througth 15. In verses 3 through 5, he describes God marching in splendor to Sinai (Mount Paran, Deut. 33:2) and then to Teman, a city in Edom, as He moves toward the land of Canaan. He defeats the pagan nations along the way, flashing like sunrise, shaking the earth, splitting the mountains. In verses 8 through 15, the prophet describes the opening of the Red Sea at the Exodus and of the Jordan River when Israel entered Canaan. The great victory of Deborah and Barak is in verse 10 (Judg. 4–5), and Joshua's victory at Gibeon in verse 11 (Josh. 10). The prophet seems to look ahead in the next four verses and sees the Jews being delivered from their exile in Babylon and returning to their land. Jeremiah had written about this (Jer. 25:8–14; 29:10).

Habakkuk received these words with great fear and trembling, but their message put strength into his soul and deepened his faith, for he said, "I will wait patiently for the day of calamity to come" (v. 16). Even though the invasion would wipe out the crops, the sheep and the cattle, he said, "I will rejoice in the LORD; I will be joyful in God my Savior" (v. 18). Even a complete economic collapse would not keep him from rejoicing in the Lord. Instead of groaning in the depths of despair, he was "treading on the heights" (v. 19) like a deer, because God Almighty enabled him. His testimony is one of the great confessions of faith found in the Bible.

A Change of Heart

God didn't change, the circumstances didn't change, the Babylonians didn't change, but *the prophet changed!* Habakkuk realized that his defeat hadn't been the result of unanswered questions but of unexercised faith. He was looking at God through the circumstances instead of looking at the circumstances through the eyes of faith. When he did that, everything fell into place. He looked back and saw the greatness of God, and he looked ahead and realized that nothing was too hard for the Lord.

The prophet may have had "intellectual problems," but he learned to accept the fact of evil in the world. Facts are facts and he accepted them. *But faith is faith!* He also learned again that God is great enough even to use man's wickedness to magnify His own righteousness. His chastening of His people was an act of love, and He would accomplish His purposes, no matter how terrible the situation might be. Surely the Hebrew exiles read and discussed his book as they lived in Babylon, and surely it gave them faith and courage.

Habakkuk moved from worrying in the valley of defeat to singing on the mountains of victory because he waited on the Lord, listened to the Word and exercised faith in the Lord.

"But my righteous one will live by faith" (Heb. 10:38).

10

Nehemiah, the Leader

Blessed are the balanced.

If ever a servant of the Lord deserved a diamond-studded platinum and gold medal for persistence in finishing a tough job in a dangerous place, that person is Nehemiah. He gave up a comfortable and influential job as cupbearer to the king of Persia to go to the ruined city of Jerusalem where he rebuilt the walls and reset the gates so the city could get moving again. A servant on the staff of a fashionable oriental court is probably the last person you would choose for such a hazardous task, but the Lord knew what He was doing.

Nehemiah stands out as one of the finest leaders in the gallery of Bible successes, and books have been written about the leadership principles that guided him. However, I want to focus on only one aspect of his life and ministry and that is his *balance*. Many so-called leaders are great cheerleaders but terrible quarterbacks, excellent public speakers but failures in personal relationships. Nobody can excel in everything, but most of us can work at balancing things so that the job gets done. Nehemiah did a marvelous balancing act with six pairs of ingredients that together brought him success.[1]

Balancing the Old and the New

One of the first things we notice is that the governor knew how to balance the *old* and the *new*, a skill especially needed today. Some highly vocal leaders in the younger generation are convinced that nothing really happened until they came along, and the sooner the "old fogeys"[2] are eliminated, the better off the church will be. Like the ancient Athenians, their battle cry is, "Give us something new!" (Acts 17:21).

But if they paid attention to their Bibles, they would discover that there really isn't anything "new." Things just seem new because either we have bad memories or just haven't paid attention to history. "What has been will be again, what has been done will be done again; there is nothing new under the sun," wrote Solomon. "Is there anything of which one can say, 'Look! This is something new?' It was here already, long ago; it was here before our time" (Eccl. 1:9–10).

In *The Life of Reason*, philosopher George Santayana wrote, "Those who do not remember the past are condemned to repeat it." People forget that not only the gospel message but the whole Word of God was handed down to us from the past (1 Cor. 15:1–8), and that believers today are to take this truth and pass it on to others (2 Tim. 2:2).

A young man phoned me and shared a "brilliant idea" he had for youth evangelism. After explaining it to me, he asked, "Do you think it will work?" I said, "It always has. We did it fifty years ago in Youth for Christ and it worked." He was shocked, but it wasn't his fault that he was born too late. Whoever first said, "The ancients have stolen all our best ideas" must have been reading Ecclesiastes.

Nehemiah lived in the present but deeply respected the past. He loved his nation Israel and wept over the ruins of Jerusalem and the ridicule the Gentiles cast on the holy city day after day. Remember that Nehemiah did not rebuild the walls to glorify the past, *but to guarantee the future!* His nation had been chosen by God to accomplish great things in bringing the Scriptures and the Savior into our world, for "salvation is from the Jews" (John 4:22). The holy land and the city of Jerusalem are the stage God chose for the greatest events and the most serious decisions that would ever occur on earth.

In an era when a new generation ignores the great hymns, relegates the senior saints to basement rooms and ignorantly claims to have invented everything new, we need more people like Nehemiah. When he heard the bad news about his people, he sat down and wept, knelt down and prayed, *and then got up and worked!* Why? Because he appreciated the past and wanted to share it with future generations.

Nehemiah believed in walls. The word is used thirty-two times in his book. The walls of Jerusalem meant protection and peace for the inhabitants. The Israelites were precious to the Lord, His special treasure (Deut. 7:6; 14:2), and He wanted them to be safe. The city walls and gates also bore witness to other nations that Jerusalem was a separated city, housing a special people who belonged

to the Lord God Jehovah. When Nehemiah had the
gates closed and guarded for the Sabbath, he used God's
ancient law to teach that lesson to both the Jews and the
Gentiles (9:14; 10:31; 13:15–22). A city without walls
and gates can easily be attacked by all sorts of enemies,
and a church without respect for God's truth will soon
have no walls at all. Anything can get in, and it usually
does. A congregation without an appreciation for their
past gradually tears down the spiritual walls of the church
and jeopardizes their future.

I can imagine some Jewish youths watching the people
working on the wall and thinking to themselves, "Why
go to all this work? This is an old city. Let's get a better
location, closer to a good river, and build a new city out
of new materials." But that wasn't God's plan. God never
rejects anything just because it's old, or automatically bless
it just because it's new. Whether it's a calf or a puppy, an
ear of corn or a rose, God's pattern is to bring the new
out of the old. Let's remind ourselves that every faithful
congregation in our world today traces its ancestry to an
old man and his wife in Ur (Gen. 11:31–12:5) as well as
to one hundred and twenty Jewish believers in an upper
room in Jerusalem (Acts 1–2). New, indeed!

Before leaving this topic, I want to point out that
two men named Joiada and Meshallam repaired the
Jeshanah Gate (3:6; 12:39). The Hebrew word Jeshanah
is also translated "old"—this was the "Old Gate." Hurrah
for Joiada and Meshallum! In our "throwaway" society,
we usually dispose of things that are old but still useful;
in fact, manufacturers build obsolescence into almost
every product. One of our national domestic problems

is finding ways to dispose of all this obsolete material. Some nations, and at least one state in the USA, have laws permitting the "disposal" of "obsolete" people who are too old to be "useful." Where will it end?

Balancing the Word and Prayer

Nehemiah also knew how to balance the *Word of God* and *prayer*, antedating the apostles in the early church, who said, "We . . . will give our attention to prayer and the ministry of the word" (Acts 6:4). These are the essentials for an effective ministry that glorifies the Lord. Moses met God on the mountain or in his private tabernacle (Exod. 33:7–11), interceded for the nation and then taught God's Word to the people in the camp. Samuel had the same burden: "As for me, far be it from me that I should sin against the LORD by failing to pray for you. And I will teach you the way that is good and right" (1 Sam. 12:23). Jesus taught His disciples the Word and prayed for them, and told them (and us) in John 15:7, "If you remain in me and my words remain in you, ask whatever you wish, and it will be done for you." Paul also depended on the Word and prayer (2 Thess. 3:1; Eph. 6:17–18; Col. 4:2).

Nehemiah invited the noted Old Testament scholar Ezra to bring the Book of the Law to Jerusalem and conduct a Bible conference for the people (Neh. 8). The law of God is mentioned twenty-one times in this book. It was during this time of exposition that the people discovered they were supposed to celebrate the Feast of Booths during the seventh month, and they did so (8:13–18). Nehemiah 9 is a review of the history of Israel, and chapter 10 records how the Scriptures brought conviction to the people's hearts and they willingly dedicated themselves anew to the Lord. It's not our clever ideas but the Word of God that revives and cleanses God's people. The Law of Moses also revealed to Nehemiah that there were people in the Jewish assembly who didn't belong there, so they were dealt with and dismissed (13:1–3, 23–28). Nehemiah obeyed God's Word and God blessed him (see Ps. 1:1–3).

Though he lived in a foreign land and among a pagan people, Nehemiah knew the Word of God (1:8–9); and when he went to Jerusalem to serve, he took it with him in his heart and possibly in his hand. Experience and education are essential to competent leadership, but it's the Word of God that the Spirit of God uses to prepare us to serve God and His people. "All Scripture is God-breathed and is useful for teaching, rebuking, correcting and training in righteousness, so that all God's people may be thoroughly equipped for every good work" (see 2 Tim. 3:14–17). The Bible doesn't just enlighten us and encourage us; it also equips us to do the job.

There must be balance if there is to be blessing. If we have all Bible and no prayer, we have light without heat; and if we have all prayer but no Bible, then we have heat without light, zeal without knowledge. When the prophet Daniel learned about the Babylonian exile from the Book of Jeremiah, he humbled himself and prayed for God to keep His promise (Dan. 9). The Word helps us to pray, and our prayers help us better understand the Word. Nehemiah could address the king on earth because he knew how to approach the King in heaven.

Twelve occasions of prayer are mentioned in the Book of Nehemiah (1:5–10; 2:4; 4:4, 9; 5:19; 6:9, 14; 9:4–19; 13:14, 22, 29, 31). Two of these prayers are a bit longer, but certainly not tedious, and the rest are like brief e-mails sent off quickly to the throne of God. Certainly Nehemiah was a man of prayer, and his longer prayers in private provided the power for the "telegraph prayers" he sent while directing the work.

Balancing Vision and Knowledge

Nehemiah also balanced *vision* with *knowledge*. God gave him the vision for rebuilding the walls of Jerusalem, but that wasn't enough. After Nehemiah arrived on the scene, he made an undercover survey of the ruins of the city late one night (2:11–20), because there is nothing like firsthand information when you are going to deal with a serious problem. When he challenged the Jewish leaders to rebuild the city walls, he knew what he was talking about, and they agreed to work together with him to get the job done.

It's important that we survey the situation with the eyes of faith and not just with the eyes of human assessment. Of the twelve spies that Moses sent to survey the land of Canaan, ten of them had no faith at all; only Joshua and Caleb believed that the Canaanites were the grasshoppers and the Israelites were the giants (Num. 13). Led by the ten unbelieving spies, the nation set the conquest of Canaan back thirty-eight years! The twelve apostles didn't have enough money to buy bread for five thousand hungry people, and they didn't see how a little boy's lunch could feed everybody; but Jesus solved the problem by trusting the Father (John 6:1–15). Unbelief sees the obstacles, but faith sees the opportunities (1 Cor. 16:8–9). God-given vision is very important as we serve (John 4:35), but the eyes of the heart must also be opened by faith if we are to see things as God sees them (Eph. 1:17–23).

Someone has defined a committee as a group of people who individually can do nothing and collectively decide that nothing can be done. That definition may not be true of every committee, but it's true enough times to bring discouragement to leaders. When the Lord calls us to do a job, He usually gives us enough challenges to excite us, enough problems to humble us and enough promises to keep us trusting and working. Faith doesn't mean we ignore the facts; it just means we see them and weigh them from God's viewpoint. It's interesting how many remarkable things people have accomplished that the experts said couldn't be done!

Don't be afraid of the facts. The more you know about your situation, the better you can pray and the wiser you will be in handling problems. Young David didn't ask Goliath how tall he was. He just knew that God was bigger and acted accordingly. The early church didn't hold a protest meeting or try to bribe the guards when Peter was in prison. They simply met together and prayed together late into the night, and the Lord delivered Peter (Acts 12). Facts are facts and faith is faith, and the two meet in the hearts of people who know the Word and know how to pray.

Balancing Leading and Serving

Nehemiah was both a *leader* and a *servant*, and this balance is important to effective service for the Lord. Nehemiah didn't sit in a comfortable office and issue orders; rather, he was on the job day and night, doing his share of the work and taking his share of the risks. No leader can do the job alone, and no worker wants to follow an absentee leader. That's why our Master said to us, "And surely I am with you always, to the very end of the age" (Matt. 28:20). By His Holy Spirit, our Lord works in us and through us to accomplish His purposes in this world (Eph. 2:10; Phil. 2:12–18). We lead by serving and we serve by leading.

As the king's appointed governor, Nehemiah could have exercised authority and enjoyed all the special privileges his assignment entailed, but he chose not to. He stayed with the workers (4:21–23), dealt personally with the people who were selfishly taking advantage of others (5:1–13) and refused to take the special allowances that were rightfully his (5:14–19). He not only paid for his own food, but he shared what he had with hundreds of others. Nehemiah willingly laid aside his rights for God's glory and for the good of the suffering people, and God honored him for it. He would not have mentioned this fact publicly except that he had to expose and embarrass the Jews who were exploiting the poor people instead of assisting them. He was an example to everyone of sacrifice and service (Phil. 2:17–18).

While serving at court as the king's cupbearer, Nehemiah had no doubt seen plenty of royal splendor and wasteful extravagance, and it grieved his heart. His greatest honor was to be the servant of the Most High God, and he refused to use his position to promote himself. Yes, he was their leader, but he was a leader who served and a servant who led—by his own example. He was like our Lord Jesus Christ, who said to His disciples, "I am among you as one who serves" (Luke 22:27). By being a humble servant (Phil. 2:5–13), Jesus set the example for all of us who belong to Him and seek to serve Him.

Balancing Building and Guarding

Nehemiah knew the importance of both *building* and *guarding*: if he didn't protect what he had built, the enemy could take it from him, and his labor would have been in vain. When the enemies who surrounded Jerusalem saw that their underhanded schemes weren't working, they took a new approach: fear. They started a rumor that they would soon attack the city and stop the progress of the work (4:7–23). Some of the Jews believed this rumor and became frightened, but not Nehemiah. He posted armed guards at key places on the wall; and while half of the men worked on the wall, the other half stood guard with their spears and swords ready. The enemy finally got the message and used other tactics. Our Lord may have been thinking about this scenario when He spoke the two parables recorded in Luke 14:25–33, because they deal with building and battling. It takes both to have a successful ministry.

"To pray and not to watch is presumption," said Charles Spurgeon, "and watching without praying is equally futile."[3] Nehemiah and the people did both: "But we prayed to our God and posted a guard day and night to meet this threat . . . and each of the builders wore his sword at his side as he worked" (4:9, 18).

When Charles Spurgeon began publishing a magazine, he named it *The Sword and Trowel*, to indicate the two goals in mind: building up the saints and protecting them from the enemies of the gospel. How tragic it is when careless Christian leaders don't guard the spiritual treasures! Their unconcern only allows the Enemy to steal them (1 Tim. 6:20; 2 Tim. 1:14). While the custodians sleep, Satan and his agents capture homes, schools, churches and other Christian ministries and use them to promote his evil enterprises.

After the dedication of the walls, Nehemiah had to return to Susa and report to King Artaxerxes. When later he came back to Jerusalem, his joy turned to sorrow when he discovered that the leaders had permitted all sorts of compromises to take place, and Nehemiah had to "clean house" (13:6ff). The godly pastor of a very successful church told me, "If I took my eyes off this flock for twenty-four hours, we would be in trouble." It doesn't take long for a little yeast to leaven the whole batch of dough (1 Cor. 5:6) or for one of Satan's masqueraders (2 Cor. 11:12–15) to "slip in" among us and replace God's truth with the world's wisdom (Jude 4).

We must maintain balance. To spend all our time fighting enemies but not building the work is to win a war but have nothing to show for it. Likewise, to build a ministry but not stay alert spiritually and guard means eventually losing it. Some ministries are known only for what they fight against, while others are overly positive and never seem to oppose the enemy. Blessed are the balanced! "Peace at any price" is not a biblical strategy, because the wisdom that comes from God is first of all pure and then peace-loving (James 3:17–18).

Balancing Burdens and Blessings

Nehemiah and the Jewish people who returned to Jerusalem had to balance *burdens* with *blessings* as they lived and worked in the holy city. It was a blessing for them to be in their own land and to work in Jerusalem with people of like faith and heritage. It was a special privilege to work on the walls and gates and help beautify and fortify the one city that was closest to their hearts.

But life wasn't easy in Jerusalem and the work wasn't easy. "The strength of the laborers is giving out," said some of the people from Judah, "and there is so much rubble that we cannot rebuild the wall" (4:10). When they temporarily left the city, there was always the threat of an ambush; and if they remained in the city, perhaps the enemy troops would attack and take over. Parents had to watch their children lest they innocently investigate the construction sites and be injured. Obviously the Jews didn't have the kind of power equipment we have today and the days were long and the nights threatening. They wept when the heard the law read and explained (8:9–10), but they rejoiced when they celebrated the feasts and shared good gifts with others (8:11–18). Ever since Adam's fall, life has been made up of blessings and burdens, joys and sorrows. "Into each life some rain must fall," wrote Henry Wadsworth Longfellow, and he was right.

Thanks to faith, persistence and hard work, it took only fifty-two days to finish the walls, after which the gates were put into place (6:16–7:1). Now the leaders could start organizing the people and teaching them the proper way to worship the Lord (9:1–12:26). For the dedication of the walls, Nehemiah and Ezra organized a great service with two choirs marching and singing on the walls and then meeting to sing together. The priests read from the Law of Moses and the people rejoiced and feasted.

When Moses was preparing the new generation to enter the Promised Land, he described it as "a land of mountains and valleys that drinks rain from heaven" (Deut. 11:11). Life has its mountains and valleys, and we enjoy the spiritual "highs" in life; but you can't have mountains without valleys! We must remember that the problems of life aren't solved by looking up to the mountains *but by looking higher and seeing Jesus by faith* (Heb. 12:1–2). "I will lift up my eyes to the mountains— where does my help come from? My help comes from the Lord, the Maker of heaven and earth" (Ps. 121:1–2). God sends the "showers of blessing" (Ezek. 34:26) when we need them and "the valleys are mantled with grain; they shout for joy and singing" (Ps. 65:13).

No matter what the Enemy might say, our God is "God of the valleys" (1 Kings 20:22–28), and this includes the "valley of the shadow of death" (Ps. 23:4, NASB).

Needed: Balanced Leaders

There appears to be a leadership shortage in our world today, not only in the political arena but also in the spiritual. Experience has been replaced by experiments, and the amateurs seem to be in charge.

Nehemiah was tempted to compromise, but he didn't; and to quit, but he kept on going. Ralph Waldo Emerson wrote, "No one can cheat you out of ultimate success but yourself." Note that word "ultimate"—when it's all over, when you and I are history, when the Lord examines the records and distributes the crowns. Nehemiah had his enemies, both outside the city and within, because anybody who is given leadership and accomplishes something will have enemies. But let's not be our own worst enemy because we've allowed ourselves to get unbalanced. It's a wise thing to pray, but the Lord told Joshua to stop praying and to start disciplining a disobedient soldier (Josh. 7:10–15). Blessed are the balanced!

We live in an age of specialization, when the "general practitioner" has been replaced by the "specialist" and the "repairman" by the "technician"; and it's not going to change. Local church pastors used to be dedicated generalists, but if that's true today, they had better be surrounded by "experts" in every field from adolescence to worship.

Nobody but the Lord knew that the king's cupbearer in the citadel of Susa was a born leader *and a balanced leader*, that he would be able to recruit, motivate and direct the Jewish remnant to rebuild the walls of their holy city. Was he a generalist or a specialist? My guess is that he was a generalist in most things but a specialist in at least one thing: determination. He saw the goal and was persistent in running straight toward it and inspiring the people to follow.

"To be a leader means to have determination," said Lech Walesa, the Polish labor leader who challenged the Communist Party. "It means to be resolute inside and outside, with ourselves and with others."

Nehemiah would agree with that, and he would probably add, "And it helps to have some balance."

11

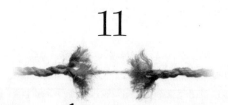

Peter, the Encourager

He cares for you.

According to Galatians 1:18, early in his Christian life, the apostle Paul spent fifteen days with the apostle Peter in the city of Jerusalem. When James McGinlay preached from that text, he used his "sanctified Scottish imagination" to visualize the two men going from place to place in the holy city and talking about Jesus.

McGinlay imagined Peter reviewing for Paul his own conversion and call to ministry, and then taking him to Gethsemane, Calvary and the garden tomb, as they talked about the death, burial and resurrection of Jesus. With pain in his heart, Peter recalled his denial of Jesus. Then they went to the Mount of Olives and reflected on the Lord's commission to the church and His ascension into heaven.

McGinlay imagined Paul asking Peter to go with him to the place where Stephen was stoned, where Paul had held the coats of the executioners (Acts 7:58–8:1). McGinlay imagined Paul saying, "Peter, when I get to heaven, I want to see my Savior first of all, and then I

want to see Stephen." The memory of Stephen's death
had stayed in Paul's mind and been used by the Lord
to prepare Saul of Tarsus to put his faith in Jesus (Acts
22:20).[1]

Paul could never forget approving the death of
Stephen, nor could Peter forget denying Jesus three
times. What the Lord said to Peter in the upper room
stayed in his heart: "Simon, Simon, Satan has asked to
sift all of you as wheat. But I have prayed for you, Simon,
that your faith may not fail. And when you have turned
back, strengthen your brothers" (Luke 22:31–32).

Yes, Peter had sinned; but Peter had been forgiven,
restored and recommissioned (John 21:19), not only to
evangelize the lost but to encourage the saved!

Think of it—Peter the encourager! Not the boaster
who failed but the failure who ultimately succeeded and
helped others to succeed. Satan wanted Peter to quit, but
the Lord's words helped to keep Peter going. Our Lord's
words to Peter tell us what we need to know to maintain
an encouraging outlook on life, so let's consider them.

We Are Weak

It must have surprised Peter, and perhaps hurt him
just a little, that three times in that upper room statement
Jesus used his old name "Simon." It was as though the
Lord was gently reminding Peter that there was still
enough of the old "Simon" left in him that he had better
be careful lest he stumble and fall. It's true that the "big
fisherman" had come a long way since that day three years
before when his brother Andrew brought him to Jesus
(John 1:40–42). During those years, he had listened to

Jesus teach, he had healed people and even raised the dead, he had walked on the water with Jesus, he had become the leader of the disciple band, and he was sure, very sure, that he knew how be a successful Christian. Courage and self-confidence were Peter's strongest qualities, and he failed miserably in both.

"Although I want to do good," wrote Paul, "evil is right there with me" (Rom. 7:21). An enthusiastic young man reported to Alexander Whyte, the godly pastor of Free St. George's in Edinburgh, Scotland, that he had attended a convention and experienced a great victory over sin. Whyte replied, "Aye, it's a sore battle up to the very last!" It was for Peter and it is for us.

How can knowing that we are weak sinners encourage us to become victorious saints? Paul gives us the answer in Second Corinthians 4:7: "But we have this treasure in jars of clay to show that this all-surpassing power is from God and not from us." Like a jeweler who displays brilliant diamonds on pieces of black felt, so God puts the treasure of eternal life into vessels of clay, so that when His power works through us, people will be amazed and ask, "How did that happen?" Peter the fisherman preaches a powerful sermon, heals a man crippled from birth, restores a paralyzed man, raises a woman from the dead—how did these things happen? "We have this treasure in jars of clay" so that God receives all the glory.

"Their sins and lawless acts I will remember no more," says the Lord concerning His people (Heb. 10:17; Jer. 31:34), and we should rejoice in that—but we should never forget Psalm 103:14: "he remembers that we are dust." Paul wrote, "So if you think you are standing firm, be careful that you don't fall" (1 Cor. 10:12). "I am ready to go with you to prison and to death," Peter boasted, and this was the beginning of his fall. He forgot that he was made of clay.

"For when I am weak, then I am strong" (2 Cor. 12:10).

Satan Is on the Prowl

"Simon, Simon, Satan . . ."

I'm not so sure I would appreciate having my name that closely associated with the devil, but it wasn't the first time Jesus had connected the two. When Peter heard Jesus announce that He would be arrested in Jerusalem and crucified, Peter protested: "Never, Lord! This shall never happen to you!" Jesus replied, "Get behind me, Satan!" (Matt. 16:22–23). Get behind me, Adversary!

The word "never" was on Peter's lips more than once. In the upper room, he told Jesus, "No, you shall never wash my feet" (John 13:8), and he boasted, "Even if I have to die with you, I will never disown you" (Matt. 26:35). A few years later, when the Lord was about to send Peter to preach the gospel to the Gentiles, He showed him a vision of a sheet full of all kinds of animals, clean and unclean. The Lord said, "Get up, Peter! Kill and eat!" Peter's reply was, "Surely not, Lord! I have never eaten anything impure or unclean" (Acts 10:11–14).

In the upper room, Jesus made it clear that God was in charge and that Satan could do nothing without His permission. (See Job 1–2.) The metaphor Jesus used was that of a farmer sifting his grain: the grain would drop through the sieve but the chaff would remain and be thrown away. Satan sifted the eleven disciples but not Judas, for the Evil One was already in control of Judas (Luke 22:3; John 6:70–71). Peter would deny Christ, but Judas would betray Him and sell Him for the price of a slave.

Peter wrote two inspired epistles. The first one focuses on God's grace in times of persecution and warns, "Be alert and of sober mind. Your enemy the devil prowls about like a roaring lion looking for someone to devour" (1 Pet. 5:8). The second letter emphasizes the dangers of false teachers, ministers of Satan who stealthily get into churches and spread their lies (2 Cor. 11:1–4, 13–15, and see 2 Pet. 2). The serpent deceives and the lion devours; if the one approach doesn't work, he tries the other; and we must be awake and alert to detect his strategy.

We don't honor the devil, but we do respect him and try not to give him a foothold in our lives (Eph. 4:27). Our Lord has already defeated the devil and has given to us the equipment we need to overcome him and his hosts of demons (Eph. 6:10–20). "Now is the time for judgment on this world," said Jesus; "now the prince of this world will be driven out" (John 12:31). "For he has rescued us from the dominion of darkness and brought us into the kingdom of the Son he loves" (Col. 1:13). We don't fight *for* victory; we fight *from* victory, the victory that Jesus won in His death on the cross, His resurrection and His ascension. He reigns today in heaven and is "head over everything for the church" (Eph. 1:22). That word "everything" includes the devil.

Knowing this truth ought to motivate us to obey what Peter wrote: "Be alert and of sober mind" (1 Pet. 5:8).

Peter, James and John went to sleep in the garden while Jesus was praying. Had Peter been "alert and of sober mind," watching and praying, he could have avoided cutting off a man's ear in the garden, following the crowd to the high priest's house when Jesus said "let these men go " (John 18:8), and denying the Lord three times. Peter learned from his mistakes and believers today can learn from Peter's mistakes. If we understand the devil's devices and are equipped by the Word of God and prayer, we can defeat him in the triumphant power of Jesus.

As we read Peter's two letters, we discover how much he knew personally about suffering as a Christian. "In all this you greatly rejoice, though now for a little while you may have had to suffer grief in all kinds of trials" (1 Pet. 1:6). Christians would be called "evil doers" (2:12) and simply have to live such godly lives that nobody would believe the accusation. Christian slaves would face "unjust suffering," so Peter set Jesus Christ before them as the perfect example of enduring unjust suffering (2:18–25).

Peter also announced that a "fiery trial" was coming (4:12–19), referring to Nero's persecution of believers which began in July of 64 AD. Throughout his letters, Peter magnified Jesus Christ and reminded his readers that Christ suffered for them far beyond anything they would have to endure for Him, and that their suffering would ultimately lead to glory, as it did with Jesus (1:7; 4:13; 5:1, 4). In fact, the Holy Spirit would help them experience that glory *today* (4:14)! We should rejoice when we suffer for Jesus' sake, as did the apostles in their day (1:6; Acts 5:40–41).

Our Faith Is Under Attack

Beginning with his confession of faith recorded in Matthew 16:16—"You are the Messiah, the Son of the living God"—Peter had given a clear and courageous witness of the deity of Jesus Christ. "Lord, to whom shall we go? You have the words of eternal life. We have come to believe and to know that you are the Holy One of God" (John 6:68–69). But now Satan was attacking that witness and Jesus prayed that Peter's faith would not fail. The Greek word translated "fail" gives us our English word "eclipse." An eclipse of the sun doesn't extinguish the sun but merely covers the light temporarily. Eclipsed faith is temporary darkness until the light returns. Peter's courage failed, but not his faith; for when the rooster crowed and the Lord turned and looked at him, Peter remembered the word Jesus had spoken and "he went outside and wept bitterly" (Luke 22:62). God accepted his repentance, for "a broken and a contrite heart you, God, will not despise" (Ps. 51:17). After His resurrection the Lord met with Peter, forgave him and restored him to his ministry (1 Cor. 15:5; John 21).

The Enemy seeks to weaken and then destroy our faith, because the only way God's people can please God and live joyfully and successfully is by faith (2 Cor. 5:7; Heb. 11:6). The first statement of Satan in Scripture is an attack on our faith in God's truth: "Did God really say, 'You must not eat from any tree in the garden?'" (Gen. 3:1). That's why Peter wrote, "Resist him [Satan], standing firm in the faith . . . " (1 Pet. 5:9). If we neglect or ignore the Word of God, we are playing right into the hands of the Enemy and weakening our own faith.

"We do not want you to become lazy, but to imitate those who through faith and patience inherit what has been promised" (Heb. 6:12).

According to Peter, the faith of God's people is "precious" (2 Pet. 1:1) and enables us to be shielded by God's power and filled with glorious joy (1 Pet. 1:5, 8). Our faith is tested (1:7) but it endures, because it is grounded in the finished work of Christ and the eternal word of God (1:21). Peter said it so well in the benediction to his first letter: "And the God of all grace, who called you to his eternal glory in Christ, after you have suffered a little while, will himself restore you and make you strong, firm and steadfast" (5:10). He was speaking from experience, from his heart.

We're in This Together

If we keep in mind that we are made of clay and that we have an Enemy who targets our faith and wants us to fail, we will quickly depend on the Lord and trust Him to keep us from quitting. Let's also remember that *we are not alone in this battle.* "Resist him [Satan], standing firm in the faith, because you know that your fellow believers throughout the world are undergoing the same kind of suffering" (1 Pet. 5:9). You and I aren't the only "elect exiles" in this world (1 Pet. 1:1), and the perseverance of one believer encourages others to keep going. "In fact, everyone who wants to live a godly life in Christ Jesus will be persecuted" (2 Tim. 3:12).

One of Satan's most insidious tactics is to try to make us believe that we're alone in the battle and that neither the Lord nor His people know our needs or care how we feel. "I am like a desert owl, like an owl among the ruins," wrote David. "I lie awake; I have become like a bird alone on a roof" (Ps. 102:6–7). "Look and see, there is no one at my right hand; no one is concerned for me. I have no refuge; no one cares for my life" (Ps. 142:4).

Peter's answer to David is, "Cast all your anxiety on him because he cares for you" (1 Pet. 5:7). God cares and other believers care! When God's people care for each other, it's evidence that God cares for them. "Truly I tell you," said Jesus, "whatever you did for one of the least of these brothers and sisters of mine, you did it for me" (Matt. 25:40). We are not alone in the battle, and we must remember to minister to others, even as they remember to minister to us. It was when Elijah the prophet was alone that he was ready to give up and quit the battle and even asked God to take his life (1 Kings 19). "At my first defense, no one came to my support, but everyone deserted me," wrote Paul. "But the Lord stood at my side and gave me strength" (2 Tim. 4:16–17). "And surely I am with you always, to the very end of the age" (Matt. 28:20).

The British Bible expositor G. Campbell Morgan once visited two elderly sisters and gave that phrase to them for an encouragement, saying, "Isn't that a wonderful promise?" One of the sisters spoke up, "It is not a promise! It's a fact!" Our enjoyment of His presence may be conditional, but the assurance of His presence is not conditional.

Some years ago, my wife and I were going through a "fiery furnace" of testing that could have crippled our ministry, if not destroyed it. I had a phone call from a well-known pastor, a friend whom I rarely phoned, and he wanted to know how things were going. I shared the burden with him, he gave me some excellent words of encouragement and then prayed for us, and the conversation was over. *But the blessing continued for days!* By what he did, he reminded us that we weren't alone on the battlefield and that there was no reason for us to be discouraged.

Jesus Is Praying for Us!

Peter's next encouragement should especially thrill our hearts: *Jesus prayed for Peter and He is praying for us today!*

Jesus prayed all night before He called the twelve disciples (Luke 6:12–16), which means He made no mistake when he included Peter and Judas Iscariot. Throughout His ministry Jesus prayed for the apostles, and before He went to the cross, He prayed not only for them but also *for His church today* (John 17). Today, Jesus is interceding for us in heaven. "Therefore he is able to save completely [forever] those who come to God through him, because he always lives to intercede for them" (Heb. 7:25). Redemption is His finished work on earth, and intercession is His unfinished work in heaven. On earth He died for sinners; in heaven He lives to intercede for the saints. "I pray for them. I am not praying for the world, but for those you have given me, for they are yours" (John 17:9).

The Holy Spirit who dwells within us is also interceding for us, for

. . . the Spirit helps us in our weakness. We do not
know what we ought to pray for, but the Spirit himself
intercedes for us through wordless groans. And he who
searches our hearts knows the mind of the Spirit, because
he intercedes for God's people in accordance with the
will of God. (Rom. 8:26–27)

When our prayers are not in agreement with God's
will, the Holy Spirit "edits" them and aligns them with
God's will, and then He seeks to teach us what God's will
is. The Spirit's ministry is something like the automatic
pilot that helps to keep a plane on course. Sometimes the
Spirit even stops us from praying about a certain matter
because He knows our request is contrary to the Father's
will.

But we must pray also! Twice our Lord told His
disciples in the garden, "Pray that you will not fall into
temptation"(Luke 22:40, 46). However, instead of praying,
they went to sleep; and when they were awakened, they
made one mistake after another.

Because Jesus and the Holy Spirit are constantly
interceding for us, we can obey First Thessalonians
5:16–18: "Rejoice always, pray continually, give thanks
in all circumstances; for this is God's will for you in
Christ Jesus." If we are walking in the Spirit (Gal. 5:16)
and fixing our attention and affection on things above,
where Christ is interceding for us (Col. 3:1–2), then the
"connection" between us and heaven and is complete and
the Lord's power can work in and through us. As long as
we are "praying in the Holy Spirit" (Jude 20), the Word
is nourishing us and the fellowship of God's people is

encouraging us, then we can bring glory to God and do His will on earth.

Repent and Be Restored

Disobedience is not a dead end street; it's more of a cul-de-sac that provides space for us to turn around. Jesus said, "And when you have turned back, strengthen your brothers" (Luke 22:32). "My dear children, I write this to you so that you will not sin. But if anybody does sin, we have an advocate with the Father—Jesus Christ, the Righteous One" (1 John 2:1). As our High Priest, Jesus can give us the grace we need to overcome temptation (Heb. 4:14–16); but if we fall, He is our Advocate and will forgive us and restore us, if we confess our sins.

Satan is very subtle in his attacks. As we are being tempted, he says, "You deserve to enjoy this sin, and I guarantee that you can get away with it." If we believe him and sin, then he says, "You can't get away with this! God has rejected you! Give up!"

But Jesus says that we can be restored.

Peter reminds us of this glorious truth in that magnificent benediction in his first epistle: "And the God of all grace, who called you to his eternal glory in Christ Jesus, after you have suffered a little while, will himself restore you and make you strong, firm and steadfast" (1 Pet. 5:10). In Peter's day the word translated "restore" was a medical term for setting a broken bone; it was also a fisherman's word for mending and preparing nets (Mark 1:19). You *can* walk again! You *can* go fishing again! Whatever you do, *don't quit!*

Peter didn't lose his salvation because of his sin, but

he did temporarily lose his fellowship with the Lord. At the empty tomb, the angel said to the women, "He has risen! He is not here. See the place where they laid him. But go, tell his disciples and Peter ..." (Mark 16:6–7). It's generally believed that John Mark wrote his gospel with the help of Peter, so those words "and Peter" are significant. Jesus met with Peter and restored him to fellowship and discipleship (1 Cor. 15:3–5; John 21:15–19).

"Brothers and sisters, if someone is caught in a sin, you who live by the Spirit should restore that person gently" (Gal. 6:1). The word "restore" is the same word we met in 1 Peter 5:10 and Luke 22:32—to set a broken bone, to mend a net. When he was a fisherman, how many times had Peter mended his nets so he could go back out on the Sea of Galilee and catch fish? Jesus wasn't through with Peter, nor is Jesus through with us.

Restored to Serve Others

"And when you have turned back, strengthen your brothers," Jesus said to Peter (Luke 22:32), and He says it to us today. Satan wanted Peter to feel permanently damaged and therefore disqualified from the ministry, but Jesus had other plans. Peter's own experience of failure, forgiveness and restoration had taught him much about the grace of God, and this helped to equip him for pastoral service to others.

I opened this chapter with a reference to the visit Paul made to Peter in Jerusalem early in his ministry (Gal. 1:18), and I want us to return to it. Paul was a highly educated Jew and a trained rabbi, while Peter was a fisherman whose schooling was limited, *yet they were one in Christ and could enjoy spiritual fellowship!* Paul the rabbi listened to Peter the fisherman as he shared what he had experienced with Jesus during those years of discipleship. Paul had seen Christ in heavenly glory and heard Him speak (Acts 9:1–19), but Peter shared what he had learned from the Master when He was ministering on earth. They strengthened one another.

When you read the lists of the names of the apostles in the Gospels and Acts, you notice that Peter's name is always first. He was first among equals in the disciple band and exercised spiritual leadership during the early years of the church (Acts 1–12). From Acts 13 to 28, the focus is on Paul, although Peter has a very important cameo appearance in 15:7–11. Peter "the rock" was an important part of the "foundation of the apostles and prophets" on which Christ is building His church.

Peter also strengthened young John Mark whom he had led to faith in Christ (1 Pet. 5:13). After the Lord delivered Peter from prison, he had gone to Mark's mother's house where a group of believers was interceding for him (Acts 12:1–17). Mark was probably there and must have marveled at what God had done for Peter. John Mark served with his cousin Barnabas and with Paul for a time, but then he left them and returned home (Acts 12:25–13:13). When Barnabas wanted to take Mark on the second missionary journey, Paul adamantly refused, and the "team" broke up; but Barnabas took his young cousin and taught him how to serve (Acts 15:36–41). Paul was concerned about the work, while Barnabas was concerned about the worker, but they couldn't see each other's point of view. However, Mark learned to serve effectively and ended up working with both Peter and Paul (1 Pet. 5:13; 2 Tim. 4:11).

When you read Peter's two epistles, you learn that he was sensitive to the needs of others, ready to give encouragement and always seeking to glorify Jesus Christ. In the first eleven verses of his second letter, Peter encourages us to draw upon God's power and grow spiritually, for "if you do these things, you will never stumble" (2 Pet. 1:10). Peter knew something about stumbling. His first epistle tells us how to handle persecution and "suffer according to the will of God" (4:19) so that our trials will purify and edify the church and glorify God. "The end of all things is near. Therefore be alert and of sober mind so that you may pray. Above all, love each other deeply, because love covers over a multitude of sins" (4:7–8).

It's unfortunate that well-meaning but misguided Christians have so emphasized Peter's failings that we have almost forgotten his achievements. Shame on us! The church owes a great deal to Peter and the encouragement he has given to God's people over the centuries. "Remember your leaders, who spoke the word of God to you. Consider the outcome of their way of life and imitate their faith" (Heb. 13:7–8).

Like Peter, let's be encouragers.

12

Paul, the Perfecter

Keep growing and you can keep going.

T o consider persons and events and situations only in the light of their effect upon myself is to live on the doorstep of hell."

Those words arrested my attention as I began to read chapter 3 of Thomas Merton's best-selling book *No Man Is an Island*.[1] I paused and read them again. At my request a friend made them into an attractive plaque which I have in my study, just under the clock. I read it several times a day. The statement has encouraged me many times and convicted me many more times, but I have no plans to remove the plaque. People, events and situations can be either irritating or irrigating, opportunities or obstacles, depending on how I handle them. However, I haven't yet achieved the level the apostle Paul reached: "I have learned to be content whatever the circumstances" (Phil. 4:11).

Never Stop Growing

Answering his accusers who boasted that they were superior to Paul, the apostle wrote:

Are they servants of Christ? (I am out of my mind to talk like this.) I am more. I have worked much harder, been in prison more frequently, been flogged more severely, and been exposed to death again and again. Five times I received from the Jews the forty lashes minus one. Three times I was beaten with rods, once I was pelted with stones, three times I was shipwrecked, I spent a night and a day in the open sea. I have been constantly on the move. I have been in danger from rivers, in danger from bandits, in danger from my own people, in danger from Gentiles; in danger in the city, in danger in the country, in danger at sea, and in danger from false believers. I have labored and toiled and have often gone without sleep; have known hunger and thirst and have often gone without food. I have been cold and naked. Besides everything else, I face daily the pressure of my concern for all the churches. (2 Cor. 11:23–28)

After all that suffering Paul could still write, with an inspired pen and a clear conscience, "I have learned to be content whatever the circumstances." Remarkable!

The Greek word translated "content" could be translated "contained" or "sufficient within myself." Not "sufficient *of* myself"—that would be pride—but "sufficient within myself." Paul was humbly depending on the sufficiency of Christ who by His Spirit dwells within each believer. "I can do all this through Christ who gives me strength" (Phil. 4:13). *Paul could keep going because he never stopped growing.* "Not that I have already obtained all this, or have already arrived at my goal, but I press on to take hold of that for which Christ Jesus took hold of me" (Phil. 3:12).

"I press on," Paul wrote. He was always expending

energy as he ran the race toward the one goal of Christian perfection—the kind of spiritual maturity that would enable him to finish the race successfully. He wanted to be a blessing to as many people as possible, and in all things to glorify Jesus Christ.

Not Mature, but Maturing

The person who says, "I'm a mature Christian" probably ought to say, "I'm a *maturing* Christian," because most of us have areas in our lives that still need perfecting. A missionary said to me, "I'm tired of working with so-called mature Christians. I'd rather have *maturing* Christians who don't claim they've arrived yet." He was right, and so was Paul. None of us has yet reached the goal of complete maturity and we desperately need the Lord and each other or we never will reach it.

Paul used the Greek word *teleios* (complete, finished) to describe maturity in the Christian life. "We proclaim him [Christ], admonishing and teaching everyone with all wisdom, so that we may present everyone fully mature [*teleios*] in Christ" (Col. 1:28). He equated "becoming mature" (once again using the word *teleios*) with "attaining to the whole measure of the fullness of Christ" (Eph. 4:13). In other words, we mature spiritually as we become more and more like Christ in every area of our lives. Paul's concise spiritual autobiography in Philippians 3:1–14 makes this clear. Pause now and take time to read it.

As you read the Book of Acts and Paul's epistles, you get glimpses here and there of how the apostle Paul grew in his spiritual life. Let's start with Luke's account of Paul's conversion on the road to Damascus. "As he neared

Damascus on his journey, suddenly a light from heaven flashed around him" (Acts 9:3). It was a revelation of the glory of the Son of God who then spoke to Paul and replaced his traditional religion with personal salvation. Paul saw a light.

Some years later, Paul gave his testimony to the Jewish crowd in the temple in Jerusalem and said, "About noon as I came near Damascus, suddenly a *bright* light from heaven flashed around me" (Acts 22:6). We've moved from "a light from heaven" to "a bright light from heaven." When Paul related his conversion experience to King Agrippa, he said, "About noon, King Agrippa, I saw a light from heaven, *brighter than the sun*, blazing around me and my companions" (Acts 26:13). Note the sequence: "a light . . . a bright light . . . brighter than the sun." As Paul's spiritual insight matured over the years, he experienced the truth of Proverbs 4:18, "The path of the righteous is like the morning sun shining ever brighter till the full light of day."

But as Paul matured in the faith, he saw not only his Savior in a brighter light, but he also saw himself. As Saul of Tarsus, the scholarly rabbi, he was confident of his self-righteousness as he sought to obey the law of Moses: "in regard to the law, a Pharisee; as for zeal, persecuting the church; as for righteousness based on the law, faultless" (Phil. 3:5–6). But when he trusted Christ, God replaced Paul's self-righteousness with the righteousness of Christ, but he never lost the consciousness of what a sinner he was without Jesus. In First Corinthians 15:9 he called himself "the least of the apostles"; later as a prisoner in Rome he wrote, "Although I am less than the least of all the Lord's people" (Eph. 3:8); and in First Timothy 1:15 he wrote, "Christ Jesus came into the world to save sinners—of whom I am the worst." What a sequence! "I am the least ... I am less than the least ... I am the worst"! The closer we get to the light, the clearer we see the dirt.

Paul also grew in his understanding of the grace of God. He always emphasized that we are saved by grace (Eph. 2:8–10) and that we serve the Lord only by His grace (1 Cor. 15:9–10). We are able to make sacrifices because of His grace at work in our lives (1 Cor. 8:1). We "reign in life" through grace (Rom. 5:17) and are able to use our suffering for God's glory because His grace is sufficient in every situation (2 Cor. 12:1–9). Our worship depends on God's grace (Col. 3:16) and so does our speaking (Col. 4:6), and the strength we need for life and service comes only from God's grace (2 Tim. 2:1). Paul never hesitated to remind his readers that there is no end to God's grace and no way to measure it! God's grace is incomparable (Eph. 2:7) and glorious (Eph. 1:6); it had been poured out abundantly on Paul (1 Tim. 1:14), and all that he was and did depended wholly on the riches of God's grace (Eph. 1:7).

No wonder Paul wrote, "But by the grace of God I am what I am" (1 Cor. 15:10).

Keep Going, Keep Growing

Three times in his epistles Paul uses the Greek word *prokope*,[2] which means "pioneer advance." It describes the work of the company of soldiers who went before the army and opened the way for them. In Philippians

1:12 it describes the advance of the gospel into places in Rome where it had never gone before, such as in Caesar's household (Phil. 4:22). In Philippians 1:25 Paul admonished the saints in Philippi to make progress in their faith; and Paul wrote to his associate Timothy, "Be diligent in these matters, give yourself wholly to them, so that everyone may see your progress" (1 Tim. 4:15). Paul had assigned Timothy to replace him as the overseer of the church in Ephesus, quite a challenge for such a young man; but all Paul was looking for was *mature spiritual development.* As God's shepherds, both Paul and Timothy had to keep growing or they could not keep going.

Our growing older doesn't guarantee that we are automatically growing up. It's tragic when people confuse age with maturity, because age records length of life while maturity relates to depth of experience and character, no matter how old we are. Alas, there are old fools as well as young fools! As we grow older, if we want to keep going, we must acquire not only practical knowledge but also spiritual wisdom. Our goal is *prokope*—pioneer advance, moving into new territory, discovering more and more of what we have in Christ and His Word.

In his second letter to Timothy, Paul wrote, "And the things you have heard me say in the presence of many witnesses entrust to reliable people who will also be qualified to teach others" (2 Tim. 2:2). This is the biblical basis for Christian preaching, teaching, mentoring and publishing, for the church of Jesus Christ is always one generation short of extinction. If we disobey this admonition, we vote for failure.

Note that verb "entrust." We are stewards of the truth

God has given us, and we must be *faithful* stewards and invest this truth in the lives of others. "Now it is required that those who have been given a trust must prove faithful" (1 Cor. 4:2). We must give the "babies" their milk so they can grow in grace and knowledge (1 Pet. 2:2; 2 Pet. 3:18), but we must not ignore the maturing saints who have grown to appreciate the meat of the Word (Heb. 5:11–14; 1 Cor. 3:1–4). "We do, however, speak a message of wisdom among the mature" (1 Cor. 2:6). Jesus commissioned Peter to feed both the lambs and the sheep (John 21:15–17).

I fear that the words of Amos 8:11 are being fulfilled today, and there is in the churches "a famine of hearing the words of the Lord." Expository Bible preaching and teaching have been replaced by film clips, dramas, topical sermons and "devotional talks" containing about as much biblical doctrine as a greeting card. The ministry of the local church is to "present everyone fully mature in Christ" (Col. 1:28), and this involves hard work! "To this end," wrote Paul, "I strenuously contend with all the energy Christ so powerfully works in me" (Col. 1:29). When pastors waste time all week pursuing the trivial, and at the last minute get a sermon outline from an on-line source, there isn't much hope that the congregation will be fed and their needs met.

"Therefore every teacher of the law who has been instructed about the kingdom of heaven is like the owner of a house who brings out of his storeroom new treasures as well as old," Jesus told His disciples (Matt. 13:52). How much spiritual treasure have we mined from the Scriptures and deposited in our storerooms?

Spiritual Stagnation Leads to Conflicts

"Besides everything else, I face daily the pressure of my concern for all the churches" (2 Cor. 11:28). That was Paul's greatest burden. Not shipwrecks and beatings and bandits, but believers, God's own people and the trouble they can cause when they get out of the will of God.

For example, the legalistic believers in the Galatian churches were "biting and devouring each other" (Gal. 5:15). The quarrel between two ladies in Philippi was in danger of splitting the church (Phil. 4:2–3). Some of the believers in Colosse were designing their own brand of Christianity by blending the gospel with gnosticism, oriental mysticism and Jewish legalism. Some of the believers in Ephesus were starting to live like the people who worshiped Diana.

But the problems in the church at Corinth outweighed them all. The church was split four ways (1 Cor. 1:10–17), and believers were using the public gatherings as occasions for showing off their spiritual gifts rather than for the edifying of the church. Some people were getting drunk at church suppers, while other members were suing each other before pagan judges. This would be enough to challenge any pastor!

What was wrong with the church at Corinth? They had been "enriched in every way" with spiritual gifts (1 Cor. 1:4–7), yet they spent their time quarreling and competing (1:10–11). Paul had shepherded them for eighteen months, but they didn't seem to know the basic truths of the Christian faith. Paul exposed their basic problem when he called them "mere infants in Christ" (3:1). In spite of all the privileges God had given them, *the believers in Corinth had stopped growing spiritually.* To them the Christian life was fun and games, being important, not being useful. They used their spiritual gifts as toys to play with and weapons to fight with instead of tools to build with. They had abandoned the apostolic injunction, "Everything must be done so that the church may be built up" (1 Cor. 14:26).

By nature little children are competitive, selfish and demanding. One of the most difficult tasks parents have is that of teaching children how to love one another, respect authority, share possessions and serve others. Spiritual "parents" face similar challenges, only without as many opportunities to enforce the lessons as biological parents have. We read First Corinthians 13 and forget that it wasn't written for weddings or funerals but *for church business meetings.* Paul was saying to them, "Why can't you learn to love one another? Why don't you put away childish things and start growing up? When I became a man, I put away childish things—and so can you!"

Paul's great desire was that the people in the churches mature. "Brothers and sisters, stop thinking like children. In regard to evil, be infants, but in your thinking be adults" (1 Cor. 14:20). The four-year-old son of a couple we know asked his father, "Daddy, where was I before I was here?" His father gave him an answer that satisfied the boy's curiosity and the matter ended. A child can occasionally come up with profound questions like that one, but that isn't the same as thinking like an adult all day long. For the most part, children focus on "What can I get?" while mature people ask, "What can I give?" We're grateful when they start to change.

Paul was a giver. "After all, children should not have to save up for their parents, but parents for their children. So I will very gladly spend for you everything I have and expend myself as well" (2 Cor. 12:14–15). A statement that Jesus had made that isn't recorded in any of the four Gospels was quoted by Paul in Acts 20:35, "It is more blessed to give than to receive." He compared his ministry to the Old Testament drink offering (Num. 6:17; 15:1–2). "But even if I am being poured out like a drink offering on the sacrifice and service coming from your faith, I am glad and rejoice with all of you" (Phil. 2:17). "For I am already being poured out like a drink offering, and the time for my departure is near" (2 Tim. 4:6). Like Jesus, Paul "poured out his life unto death" (Isa. 53:12).

If they are to succeed in life, children must learn to be patient and obedient because they trust and love their parents, not because they might be rewarded or punished. God's children have the same responsibility. Romans 13:1–10 applies not only to God's law and civic law but also to whatever rules regulate marriage, the family, life at school and even activities at work.

While conducting a Bible conference in a church, I was a guest in the home of a lovely couple with three children. On the door of the family bathroom, the parents had posted a list of instructions telling the children when they were to wash their hands, brush their teeth, etc. Instead of solving problems, the schedule frequently created problems, because without love in our hearts, rules and regulations are powerless to make us obey. They might even tempt us to disobey just to show how "grown up" we are! (Paul discusses this in Romans 7.)

A Little Help from Your Friends

Paul didn't try to serve the Lord alone but identified himself with trustworthy like-minded men and women who assisted him in his ministry. In Romans 16 he greeted by name some twenty-six people in Rome and sent them greetings from nine believers who were with him in Corinth. In six epistles Paul included Timothy in his greetings. Paul's life was spared thanks to the intervention of a nephew who told the Roman centurion about the Jewish conspiracy (Acts 23:12–22), and we don't even know the boy's name! Paul's brief letter to Philemon ("our dear friend and fellow worker") and Apphia and Archippus reveals the heart of an appreciative Christian who could not only win souls but also make friends and keep them. The letter closes with greetings from five friends who were sharing Paul's prison experience in Rome! That's friendship!

Paul had friends with him during that dangerous voyage to Rome, and when he arrived in Rome, Paul "thanked God and was encouraged" when he saw believers who had traveled out to meet him (Acts 28:14–15). The first group traveled over forty miles to meet him and the second group about ten miles. He had written to the Roman believers that he wanted to see them so that they could be "mutually encouraged by each other's faith" (Rom. 1:12), but he hadn't planned to arrive as a Roman prisoner! On more than one occasion in our itinerant ministry, my wife and I have unexpectedly met friends in a variety of places—church services, airports or airplanes, even hotel dining rooms—and have been greatly encouraged by seeing friendly faces in foreign places. It was God's extra encouragement to His travel-weary children.

Over the years I have read hundreds of biographies and autobiographies and been reminded again and again that many people succeed partly because of the encouragement and help they receive from their mates, family members, friends and work associates. I call these helpers "hinge people" because God uses them to open doors for others and point them in the right direction. Barnabas did this for Paul (Acts 11:25–26) and for John Mark (Acts 15:36–41), and Paul did it for Timothy (Acts 16:1–2).

When you consider the many "one another" admonitions in the New Testament, you discover that they can easily be summarized in this statement: "lovingly encourage one another." The Scottish preacher John Watson used to say, "Be kind, for everyone you meet is fighting a battle." For years I wrote that statement in the front of the Bibles I used for preaching, and it did me good to ponder Watson's counsel before stepping into the pulpit. After all, effective preaching simply means loving and encouraging God's people and wooing sinners by explaining and applying God's Word. God's pattern for us is "speaking the truth in love" (Eph. 4:15). It works!

"It is not good for the man to be alone" (Gen. 2:18) applies not only to marriage but also to ministry. "Two are better than one," wrote Solomon; "if they fall down, they can help each other up" (Eccl. 4:9–10). Even our Lord wanted Peter, James and John to keep watch with Him in the garden during that hour when the power of darkness attacked (Matt. 26:36–46), and Paul asked Timothy to come quickly to him in Rome and to bring John Mark with him (2 Tim. 4:9–11).

One of the greatest rewards in life is watching people succeed for whom we have prayed and to whom we have spoken words of encouragement in difficult times. Others have encouraged us and we must encourage others. Paul made a ministry out of friendship, and we should follow his example.

Suffering for the Lord

Paul suffered much during his ministry, *yet it was his suffering that helped to keep him going!* That may seem paradoxical—the Christian life is full of paradoxes—but Paul said so himself: "For when I am weak, then I am strong" (2 Cor. 12:10). In times of pain and distress, we not only learn a great deal about the Lord, but we also learn more about ourselves and what God can do for us. "We are hard pressed on every side," Paul wrote, "but not crushed; perplexed, but not in despair; persecuted, but not abandoned; struck down but not destroyed. . . . For we who are alive are always being given over to death for Jesus' sake, so that his life may also be revealed in our mortal body" (2 Cor. 4:8–9, 11). I like the paraphrase by J. B. Phillips: "knocked down but not knocked out!"

One phrase in that quotation is the key that unlocks the mystery: "for Jesus' sake."

If I suffer heroically for my own sake, I will eventually run out of fuel and give up, or if I succeed, all the praise will go to me. But if I suffer by faith for Jesus' sake and depend on His grace, I will keep going and Christ will receive the glory. To grit my teeth and bravely quote

William Ernest Henley's *Invictus*—"I am the master of my fate / I am the captain of my soul"—may bring me applause, but it won't turn my pain into power or give me a compelling reason to keep going. To suffer for nothing and nobody is the depth of physical and mental brutality, but to suffer for the highest Person—Jesus Christ—on behalf of the greatest cause—the glory of God—is the height of spiritual victory. Our own spirit may of itself be brave, but we still need the Spirit of God to give us encouragement and enablement far beyond our own ability. Strength ultimately becomes weakness when we depend on ourselves; weakness ultimately becomes strength when we depend on Jesus Christ.

From the beginning of his Christian life, Paul knew that he would pay a great price to be able to serve Jesus. God said to Ananias, "I will show him how much he must suffer for my name" (Acts 9:15–16). But God says the same thing about us: "For it has been granted to you on behalf of Christ not only to believe on him but also to suffer for him" (Phil. 1:29). When Paul and Barnabas ordained leaders in the churches they founded, they not only prayed for them but also reminded them, "We must go through many hardships to enter the kingdom of God" (Acts 14:22). When was the last time you heard a sermon on that text?

Why is it we complain and perhaps even rebel and argue with the Lord whenever suffering comes into our lives? Instead of expecting trials, and being prepared to use them for God's glory, we resent them, hide our pain and ask God to change things immediately. Sometimes we start to negotiate with our Father to see how much

He is willing to take in return for comfort and peace, when we should be praying, "Your will be done."

More than anything else, Paul wanted to reach the goal God set for him when He called him. Paul admitted that he was not yet perfected but that he was willing to let God have His way and move him closer to maturity, even if it meant suffering. "If we endure, we will also reign with him" (2 Tim. 2:12). As William Penn the Quaker said, "No pain, no palm; no thorns, no throne; no gall, no glory; no cross, no crown."

But we must keep maturing in Christ or we won't be ready for either the suffering or the glory. "However, I consider my life worth nothing to me; my only aim is to finish the race and complete the task the Lord Jesus has given me—the task of testifying to the good news of God's grace" (Acts 20:24).

If we don't keep growing, we won't keep going.

13

Timothy and Titus, the "Almost Quitters"

Stay long enough to "bloom where you're planted."

Paul, Timothy and Titus are names you soon get acquainted with as you read the Book of Acts and the New Testament epistles, but most people don't always ponder the miracle that brought these two generations together and kept them together.

Miracle?

Yes, miracle. For Paul was a "Hebrew of the Hebrews" (Phil. 3:5), Timothy had a Jewish mother but a Gentile father (Acts 16:3), and Titus was a full-blooded Gentile (Gal. 2:3). From the human point of view, this was a formula for failure. The secret of this unity was their second birth, not their first, for in Christ there is "neither Jew nor Gentile . . . for you are all one in Christ Jesus" (Gal. 3:28). They loved Jesus and they loved one another. Paul had led these two young men to faith in Christ, and God had called them into His service. They were working together for the Lord, with Paul as their mentor and leader. Timothy was in Ephesus and Titus in Crete, and both places were difficult and demanding.

Not only did these three men differ in their ethnic origin, but they also differed in personality. Paul was a courageous single-minded missionary/evangelist whose motto was "this one thing I do" (Phil. 3:13). His love for Christ compelled him to travel throughout the Roman Empire, overcoming every obstacle that he might win the lost and build up the churches. He was not ashamed of the gospel, and he was not afraid to suffer for the Lord and His people.

Timothy, on the other hand, appears to be a timid, young man who was prone to neglect his spiritual gifts (2 Tim. 1:1–7). He occasionally made impulsive decisions and was subject to "frequent illnesses" (1 Tim. 5:22–23). Conscious of his youth and inexperience, Timothy may have hesitated to give spiritual leadership to the older people in the church (1 Tim. 4:11–16; 5:1–2; 1 Cor. 16:10–11). But Paul called him a "co-worker" (Rom. 16:21; 1 Thess. 3:2), and he boasted to the believers in Philippi that he had "no one else like him, who will show genuine concern for your welfare" (Phil. 2:19–24). This was high praise, indeed, coming from Paul. Timothy loved Paul and was moved to tears when they separated at Ephesus (2 Tim. 1:4).

Titus seems to have been made of stronger stuff. When the church at Corinth faced serious problems, Paul sent Timothy to help them (1 Cor. 4:17–18; 16:10–11), but Timothy wasn't completely successful. Then Paul sent Titus who, building on Timothy's earlier ministry, got matters straightened out (2 Cor. 7:5–7; 8:16–17;

12:17–18). It's difficult to determine which of these men was in the more difficult situation: Timothy in idolatrous Ephesus or Titus ministering to the Cretans, whom even Paul admitted were "liars, evil brutes and lazy gluttons" (Titus 1:12).

But apparently both Titus and Timothy were unhappy in their ministries and wanted Paul to give them new assignments (Titus 1:5; 1 Tim. 1:3). Titus in Crete was working with difficult people who resisted his leadership as he tried to organize the churches (Titus 1:5–16), and Timothy in Ephesus was surrounded by idolatry and immorality and certainly didn't feel competent to succeed Paul in that strategic church. More than once in my own ministry I have followed men who were evangelical icons, and it wasn't easy. Timothy and Titus both had to contend with false teachers who were leading believers astray and dividing the churches, so they had difficult assignments indeed. Titus had problem people *around* him and Timothy had problems *within* him, and both felt that they needed a change.

Hang In There!

A pastor friend of mine received a new member into the church who turned out to be a gossip, a critic and a general nuisance. Whenever my friend stepped into the pulpit to preach, he saw her sitting before him, and he immediately lost the joy of the Lord. (She had attractive red hair and was easy to spot.) After enduring perhaps six months of this irritation, my friend resigned and moved to California to pastor what seemed to be an ideal church.

Guess what? He soon discovered a similar member in his new congregation, only she was a brunette.

A change in geography doesn't guarantee a solution to our problems. The grass is always greener on the other side of the fence (until you investigate and discover it's Astroturf!), and there is often a snake in what everybody thinks is a Garden of Eden. Paul knew this because he knew people and churches and how the Enemy works. But it's always too soon to quit; and the worst time for a leader to quit is when the Enemy seems to be winning. That's the time to stay and let the Lord help you fight it out. You fight the battles and your successor can claim the spoils.

I admire Timothy and Titus for at least sharing their burdens with Paul and being willing to listen to his counsel. One of the problems in churches today is that the younger generation thinks nothing really important happened until they came along, so there's no reason for them to take the advice of their elders. Titus and Timothy didn't have that attitude; they were grateful for Paul's experience and insight, and were willing to listen, learn and obey.

When you read Paul's letter to Titus and his two letters to Timothy, one of the first things you notice is Paul's positive attitude toward the work of the ministry. "I thank Christ Jesus our Lord, who has given me strength, that he considered me trustworthy, appointing me to his service" (1 Tim. 1:12). He never minimized the problems and difficulties of pastoral work, nor did he forget to give the Lord the glory for what had been accomplished. But he was happy to be a preacher of the gospel. In spite of the dangers he encountered, the sacrifices he had to make and the burdens he had to carry, Paul saw his calling as a special privilege given to him by the Lord.

Unfortunately, some ministers complain so much about their work and their people that they give the wrong impression about Christian ministry. They make it look like punishment when in reality it is spiritual nourishment. "My food," said Jesus, "is to do the will of him who sent me and to finish his work" (John 4:34). In the opening remarks to his lectures on preaching, given at Yale Divinity School back in 1877, Phillips Brooks said to the ministerial students, "I cannot begin, then, to speak to you who are preparing for this work of preaching, without congratulating you most earnestly upon the prospect that lies before you. I cannot help bearing witness to the joy of the life which you anticipate." That's the attitude that all of us must cultivate if we are to succeed in our work. Before we change addresses, we must permit God to change our attitudes.

At the same time Paul didn't suggest making their work easier so they would stay on the job. He never negotiated the will of God. He told Timothy to stay in Ephesus (1 Tim. 1:3), and he reminded Titus that he left him in Crete to get the job done (Titus 1:5). "But you, keep your head in all situations, endure hardship, do the work of an evangelist, discharge all the duties of your ministry" (2 Tim. 4:5). "Until I come, devote yourself to the public reading of Scripture, to preaching and to teaching" (1 Tim. 4:13). "Encourage and rebuke with all authority. Do not let anyone despise you" (Titus 2:15). These were not suggestions for them to consider; they were orders for them to obey. The Greek word translated "command" in the pastoral epistles is a military term that describes an order from the general handed down to the troops, an order that must be obeyed (1 Tim. 1:3, 5, 18; 4:11; 5:7, 21; 6:13, 17; 2 Tim. 4:1; Titus 1:6). "Join with me in suffering, like a good soldier of Christ Jesus" (2 Tim. 2:3). Paul never asked his associates to do anything that he wasn't doing himself.

For Timothy and Titus to abandon their assigned ministries would be to rob themselves of the spiritual growth those ministries would provide them. Ministry that builds up the church must first build up the minister. "Be diligent in these matters; give yourself wholly to them, so that everyone may see your progress" (1 Tim. 4:15). As I mentioned in an earlier chapter, the word translated "progress" means "pioneer advance," and describes the soldiers who went ahead of the main army to open the way and prepare for their arrival. To change the image, the shepherd goes ahead of the flock and leads them into fresh pastures in the Word and new opportunities for service.

The minister who changes churches every three years and turns over the barrel of sermon outlines each time may claim that he's had "fifteen years of preaching experience," but he hasn't. He's had only three years of the same experience five times. Turning over the sermon barrel isn't quite the same as blazing new trails in the Word. We need to make pioneer advance in the Word and in the development of our people in their Christian walk and work.

Passing on the Torch

Paul was not only concerned about Timothy and Titus maturing in the ministry, but he was also burdened about the future of the many churches he himself had planted. "And the things you have heard me say in the presence of many witnesses entrust to reliable people who will also be qualified to teach others" (2 Tim. 2:2). That describes four generations of Christians: Paul teaches Timothy, Timothy teaches qualified people, and those people teach others. If each generation is faithful to teach the next generation, the work of the Lord will go on; otherwise every church is only one generation short of extinction. When he wrote Second Timothy, Paul was about to be martyred, and he wanted to be certain that his "pupils" were ready to take the torch and carry on the work in his absence (2 Tim. 4:6–8).

This explains why Paul invested so much time and energy in the lives and ministries of these two men, and of many other helpers named in his letters. The pastoral epistles sent to Timothy and Titus summarize for us "how people ought to conduct themselves in God's household, which is the church of the living God, the pillar and foundation of the church" (1 Tim. 3:15). We can learn from Scripture everything we need to know about conducting the work of the church and fulfilling our own God-given ministry. There are always new tools and methods to consider, but not new spiritual principles. Paul got it right the first time.

But ministry means work! "But you, man of God . . . pursue righteousness, godliness, faith, love, endurance and gentleness. Fight the good fight of faith" (1 Tim. 6:11–

12). Expend some energy! Paul frequently used the word *doulos* and described himself as "the bond slave [servant] of Jesus Christ," because slaves have to keep doing their work and obeying their masters. "This is why we labor and strive," Paul wrote (1 Tim. 4:10), and that doesn't sound like he majored in taking naps and attending tea parties. Paul wanted Timothy to be "a worker who does not need to be ashamed" (2 Tim. 2:15). A worker!

In Second Timothy 2, Paul used several pictures of the local church to emphasize the sacrifice and service that is involved in ministry. Each church is a family ("my son," v. 1), a school (v. 2), an army (vv. 3–4), an athletic team (v. 5) and a farm (v. 6); and each of these pictures shouts, "Hard work expected here!"

The Family Metaphor

Consider the church as a family.

Like any family, the members of the church family are at different stages in age, physical development, education, training and experience. The apostle John called them "children," "young people" and "fathers" (1 John 2:12–14). They have different gifts and personalities and therefore "process life" in different ways. The babes in Christ want their milk, and we must sometimes be "nursing mothers" (1 Thess. 2:7–8; 1 Peter 2:1–3). But there comes a time when the "little children" must be weaned and introduced to the "solid food," the truths concerning the present heavenly ministry of Christ (Heb. 5:11–14). The maturing "young men and women" need to balance their zeal with knowledge and learn the spiritual disciplines of the Christian life. The "fathers and mothers" in the church family must teach the younger ones and be examples to them of believers who walk by faith. Members of a loving family minister to each other.

In First Timothy 5 and Titus 2, Paul compared the church to a family. Was young Timothy having problems with the older men and women? Then let him treat them as he would his own father and mother, and the younger members as brothers and sisters.

I began my pastoral ministry at a young age, while I was still in seminary; I followed this counsel, *and it worked!* In fact, this was my approach to ministry in all three of the churches I served. Yes, there is danger when the older people start treating the young pastor as their own son or grandchildren, but this can be dealt with in love. "The goal of this command [not to teach false doctrines] is love, which comes from a pure heart and a good conscience and a sincere faith" (1 Tim. 1:5; see also 4:12 and 6:11).

The purpose of the family is to protect the young so they can have time to learn what they need to know in order to function successfully in society. The word for it is "maturity." Just as our physical children must learn to wash themselves, clothe themselves, feed themselves, protect themselves and lovingly give themselves to help others, so the "church babies" must develop the same skills in the spiritual realm. They cannot be dependent forever (see Heb. 5:11–14). As I have prepared lessons and sermons and written books, I have tried to keep the whole church family in mind and present truths for the youngest babe as well as for the mature "senior saint."

Other Metaphors

Or consider the church as an army, fighting against the world, the flesh and the devil (Eph. 2:1–3; 6:10–18). Some people don't like the "military side" of the Christian life, but if they ignore it, they will end up defeated and disappointed. If we want to be dedicated Christians, we must expect to have enemies, because God calls us to live a counter-cultural life in a world that insists that we conform to their appetites and ambitions (2 Cor. 6:14–7:1; Rom. 12:1–2). We are marching down a narrow road which is running down the middle of a broad road crowded with people who need to listen to our message, turn around and join us (Matt. 7:13–28).

Military life isn't easy. It demands discipline, proper food and exercise, respect for authority, skill with weapons and an understanding of the ways of the enemy. "No one serving as a soldier gets involved in civilian affairs; rather, they try to please their commanding officer" (2 Tim. 2:4). From polishing shoes to mastering weapons, military people must be at their best and do their best. "Just getting by" isn't permitted when you wear a military uniform.

Let's think about the farm metaphor (2 Tim. 2:6; see also 1 Cor. 3:5–9). If anyone must work hard, it is the diligent farmer. He can prepare the soil and plant the seeds, but he can't control the weather or always overcome the destructive enemies that attack his crops, nor can he influence the market prices at harvest. If he's lazy, he reaps poverty (Prov. 24:30–34); if he's diligent and God gives him and his fellow farmers a bumper crop, he may see the prices fall radically.

My wife spent her early years on a farm in Wisconsin and loves to work in the soil. I'm grateful, because I grew up in the concrete jungles of the big city and can't distinguish a flower from a weed. I'm also grateful for the plants and flowers she cultivates out in the yard and inside the house. Over the years, she has taught me to appreciate the sacrifices and risks involved in managing a productive farm.

Just as there are seasons to farming, there are seasons in ministry. I can recall dry seasons when my own heart and the hearts of the people seemed like concrete, and then the heavens would open and the showers of blessing would come down. There have been times when I have been sitting at my desk studying or before my computer staring at the words on the screen, and I have been crying out for God's help; then the Lord sends "showers of blessing" (Ezek. 34:26), and the stream starts flowing again. Without the Lord, we can do nothing.

Whether it's the minister as parent, soldier, athlete or farmer, we're talking about work—hard work—and nothing else will do. Some of the children in the church family will break our hearts, and some of the soldiers will go AWOL or, even worse, join the enemy. (Remember Demas?) Those laps on the race track day after day may be tiring, and a few of the other runners may "succeed" by breaking the rules, but we will keep our eyes on Jesus and make it successfully to the goal. If we don't play by God's rules, there will be no reward (2 Tim. 2:5). We may plow the soil, plant the seed of the Word and water it with our prayers and tears, yet see a meager crop; but the Lord of the Harvest knows what He is doing. "Let us not become weary in doing good, for at the proper time we will reap a harvest if we do not give up" (Gal. 6:9).

When your muscles ache and your soul is weary and you feel like giving up, just remember that *you are not working alone.* If you are living by faith, feeding on the Word and yielded to the Spirit, then the Lord is working in you, through you and with you (Phil. 2:12–13; Eph. 3:20; Mark 16:20), and He will accomplish His will in ways that you and I cannot comprehend today. Keep in mind that others are also working hard in the Lord's service and that many have labored long before we arrived on the scene. Jesus quoted the proverb "One sows and another reaps" and reminded the disciples that they were entering into the labors of others (John 4:34–38). People we may not know pray for us even as we pray for others. The network of God's grace around the world is astounding and encouraging, so don't give up!

The Christian life and ministry is all a work of faith, and our faith is in Christ and His Word. Come what may, the Lord remains faithful (2 Tim. 2:13). "I thank Christ Jesus our Lord, who has given me strength" (1 Tim. 1:12). "The grace of our Lord was poured out on me abundantly" (1 Tim. 1:14).

The Importance of Leadership

Paul left Titus in Crete that he "might put in order what was left unfinished and appoint elders in every town" (Titus 1:5). The verb translated "put in order" simply means "to straighten out." "God is not a God of disorder but of peace" (1 Cor. 14:33). As I mentioned before, the church is an organism, but if an organism isn't organized, it will die. One evening, my gall bladder declared war on the rest of my body and the result was a week in the hospital that climaxed with surgery. My surgeon straightened things out and life was back to normal.

Local churches are made up of people, and people are not perfect, even Christian people. Whatever we call them—pastors, bishops, elders, deacons, church leaders—they are essential if the church body is to function effectively. Leaders must pray together, search the Scriptures together and together exercise the kind of loving biblical authority that will keep the church ministering in a healthy way that honors the Lord. *Everything rises and falls with leadership.* This explains why the Holy Spirit guided Paul to list the qualifications for church leaders in First Timothy 3 and Titus 1.

Spiritual health is the key to everything, and biblical teaching is the key to spiritual health. This is why Paul frequently mentions "sound doctrine" in his pastoral epistles; the word translated "sound" simply means "healthy." Beware of everything that is "contrary to the sound doctrine" (1 Tim. 1:10) and stick to the "pattern of sound teaching" found in Scripture (2 Tim. 1:13).

> For the time will come when people will not put up with sound doctrine. Instead, to suit their own desires, they will gather around them a great number of teachers to say what their itching ears want to hear. They will turn their ears away from the truth and turn aside to myths. (2 Tim. 4:3–4)

That time is here, and years of unfaithful church leadership is to blame. "He [the elder] must hold firmly the trustworthy message as it has been taught, so that he can encourage others by sound doctrine and refute those who oppose" (Titus 1:9). Are people going off on dangerous doctrinal detours? "Therefore rebuke them sharply, so that they will be sound in the faith. . . . You, however, must teach what is appropriate to sound doctrine" (Titus 1:13; 2:1). This approach to ministry is not popular in a society that doesn't know the truth about truth but says, "Your interpretation may be true for you, but it isn't true for me," and yet this is the approach God commands us to follow. Teach faithfully, rebuke sharply.

The emphasis in the pastoral letters is on God's servants faithfully teaching God's Word to God's people, for this is the only food we have for the healthy and the only defense we have against the devil's lies and the apostates' heresies. Church leaders must be "able to teach" (1 Tim. 3:2; Titus 2:1) and able to refute false teachers (Titus 1:9), otherwise they aren't qualified to hold office.

Biblical illiteracy and doctrinal ignorance abound in the church today. Too many believers think that all they need to keep going on the battlefield is to devote a few minutes each day to reading a Bible verse, a brief story and a poem from a daily devotional book, or perhaps halfheartedly listening to a media preacher whose theology may be unhealthy. People have time to play golf or exercise at the club, but they don't have time to train themselves to be godly (1 Tim. 4:7). They are too busy to take time to be holy.

I recall a pastor who wanted to start a church library and asked the people to contribute any suitable Christian books they were no longer using. After a few weeks he went through the pile of books that accumulated and was shocked to find that many of them were published by false cults, including the children's books! He started praying Philippians 1:10 for his people ("so that you may discern what is best . . .") and began emphasizing biblical doctrine in his messages. He hoped it wasn't too late.

Love Is the Answer

What is ministry all about?

"But the goal of our instruction is love . . ." (1 Tim. 1:5, NASB), because "knowledge puffs up while love builds up" (1 Cor. 8:1). We speak the truth in love (Eph. 4:15) so that God's people may love each other in truth (2 John 1), "for whoever loves others has fulfilled the law" (Rom. 13:8). Love and knowledge are not enemies but allies, for love prepares the way for receiving knowledge and motivates us to obey what we have learned. Paul encouraged Timothy to "pursue righteousness, godliness, faith, love, endurance and gentleness" (1 Tim. 6:11), and the word translated "pursue" is also translated "make every effort" (Rom. 14:19; Heb. 12:14).

Note that Paul connects love with endurance, as he does in Second Timothy 3:10 and Titus 2:2. The word translated "endurance" literally means "to bear up under." The weight of responsibilities, problems and difficult circumstances may press upon us, but love for God and God's people can help us persevere when we feel like dropping out. Love "always protects, always trusts, always hopes, always perseveres" (1 Cor. 13:7). Instead of thinking only of ourselves and our burdens, we think of others and how we can encourage them to keep at it.

Timothy didn't always feel at his best, but his feelings might have gotten worse had he moved to Rome or Athens. Titus was working among people who at times acted like animals, but is it easier to win people like that or polished people who cover their bestiality under a cloak of hypocrisy? In both situations the answer is love, because "love is patient, love is kind" and "love never fails" (1 Cor. 13:4, 8). Paul warned Timothy about people who were "lovers of themselves . . . lovers of pleasure rather than lovers of God" (2 Tim. 3:2, 4), and he didn't want his son in the faith to be like them.

There are no small places and *there are no easy places.* Satan the destroyer (Rev. 9:11) is hard at work trying to destroy every believer and every believing friendship, family and ministry; but God has all the grace we need to defeat the destroyer (2 Tim. 1:8–10). After all, the Lord said to Paul, "My grace is sufficient for you, for my power is made perfect in weakness" (2 Cor. 12:9).

"But he gives us more grace" (James 4:6), and never scolds us when we ask for still more!

When You Feel Like Quitting

During my years of ministry, I've occasionally been asked, "Have you ever at any time felt like quitting?" and I have had to answer honestly, "Yes, I have." The next question was usually, "How did you get the victory?" They were sometimes surprised at my answer.

First, if I'm tired, I take a nap. I've learned never to make a major decision when weary, because it will turn out to be the wrong one. If the weather isn't miserable, I might take a walk. Expending energy and breathing fresh air is helpful to the brain. (Where I live, we still have fresh air. We're fortunate.)

I ask myself if my feelings have been hurt or my pride punctured. If I've been criticized, maybe the criticism was just and I can learn from it. If not, why fret? It's impossible to please everybody and I shouldn't even try. If I can't handle it, it will all be settled when we see the Lord.

Of course, I pray about the matter and review the Scriptures I've been reading in my recent devotional times. Usually God gives me the rebuke or the promise that I need, or both. If I give myself a couple of days and keep working, the discouragement usually goes away. If not, I talk with my wife and we pray together, or perhaps I chat with a friend about the matter.

If the idea of quitting persists, I make a list of projects that must be completed before I can conveniently leave; and if they challenge me, I know God wants me to stay. Then I remind myself that it's rarely wise to *leave* a place before God has *called* you to a place, and that slows down my eagerness to get out of town.

We don't really understand our own hearts, so I'm wary of trusting my feelings, but I don't ignore them. I'm not the kind who makes instant decisions. If God really wants me to go elsewhere, He has usually made this clear over a period of time. It starts with a growing sense of detachment from the place I am serving; it's not something I work up but something the Lord seems to send down.

Usually, if God wants us to move, He has given me a definite promise or direction from the Word during my regular daily devotional time. If I find myself getting nervous and fretful, I know the devil is at work, and I take extra time for the Word and prayer.

I realize that each of us has a different way of processing life, and God accommodates Himself to our makeup, but I think this approach to the temptation to quit is a biblical and practical one.

One more thing: at some point my wife will usually smile and say to me, "It's always too soon to quit!" That has often changed my perspective.

14

Jesus, the Conqueror

You can trust your Father.

Jesus faced obstacles and enemies that would have paralyzed us, yet He was never discouraged or defeated. His greatest success looked like His greatest failure, but it was such a tremendous victory that Paul wrote, "May I never boast except in the cross of our Lord Jesus Christ . . . " (Gal. 6:14). "And having disarmed the powers and authorities, he made a public spectacle of them, triumphing over them by the cross" (Col. 2:15). What looked like tragedy was triumph.

Yet, Jesus was "a man of suffering, and familiar with pain" (Isa. 53:3), and this included the emotional pain He experienced day after day, long before He was crucified. Our Lord's forty days of conflict with the devil at the beginning of His public ministry ended with Satan the loser, but the devil "left him [Jesus] until an opportune time" (Luke 4:1, 13). Near the close of His public ministry, Jesus said to His disciples, "You are those who have stood by me in my trials" (Luke 22:28). Note that plural—"trials." The disciple band was not in existence when Jesus was tempted in the wilderness, so the Lord must have been referring to the repeated attacks of the Enemy during those "opportunities" that Satan watched for day after day. The phrase "my trials" indicates that Jesus frequently faced occasions of testing and pain never revealed to the disciples.

However, before we look at some of these occasions, we need to understand a very important fact: Jesus did not use His divine power to meet His own personal needs. *That was the very thing the devil wanted Him to do!* "You are hungry, so turn the stones into bread. You want to be popular and accepted by the crowds, so jump down from the highest point of the temple and reveal your power and glory. You have the power, so do it!"

When Jesus was serving here on earth, He met the daily attacks of the Enemy in the same way you and I must meet them today: by depending on the Holy Spirit to use the Word of God and prayer. Jesus knew God's Word and when He said "It is written," the matter was settled. In His incarnation, He had "emptied Himself" of His own independent use of His divine attributes (Phil. 2:1–11) and was wholly yielded to the Father's will. Because the Father so directed, Jesus could speak the word and calm a violent storm, but He was not directed to speak a word to silence the angry murderous religious leaders who cried, "Crucify Him! Crucify Him!" He delivered others from pain and even death, but He did not deliver Himself.

He Had Compassion

When Jesus asked His disciples who the people said He was, they replied, "Some say John the Baptist;

others say Elijah; and still others, Jeremiah or one of the prophets" (Matt. 16:14). Jeremiah was "the weeping prophet" (Jer. 9:1), so the people must have detected in the face, actions and speech of Jesus a holy empathy that showed He identified with their struggles and burdens. "When he saw the crowds, he had compassion on them, because they were harassed and helpless, like sheep without a shepherd" (Matt. 9:36). Parents put their little children in His arms, and lepers begged Him for healing. They knew that Jesus loved them and that He wanted to help them.

What did Jesus think of the world into which He had been born? Did it grieve Him that the purity, beauty and harmony of the original creation had been replaced by sin, ugliness and discord? He wept at the grave of Lazarus (John 11:35), *yet He knew He would raise him from the dead!* Why did He weep? Because He was so deeply disturbed by the ravages of sin—sickness, pain, death, separation, tears, decay—that He broke down and wept openly. Lazarus was with God; now he was coming back, only to suffer and die again someday.

When Jesus visited the "Bethesda hospital" in Jerusalem, it must have broken His heart to see the "great number of disabled people—the blind, the lame, the paralyzed" (John 5:1–4). The man Jesus healed had been an invalid for thirty-eight years! And what about the beggar who had been born blind (John 9), or the bankrupt woman who had been ill for twelve years, or the sick twelve-year-old girl who was dying at home (Luke 8:40–56)?

Yes, Jesus met their needs, but first He felt deeply the

pain and grief of all who were involved, and He knew that He would bear all of it on the cross. "Surely he took up our pain and bore our suffering" (Isa. 53:4; Matt. 8:16–17). The Hebrew verb translated "took up" in Isaiah is used in Leviticus 16:22 to describe what the scapegoat did on the annual day of atonement: "The goat will carry on itself all their sins to a remote place." The Great Physician never sent anyone a bill for His services. He paid it Himself— on the cross.

Nor did He falter or become discouraged because of the appalling conditions of the world He had created for His glory and our good. There are millions of people in today's world, many of them children, who are sick, handicapped, underfed, ill-housed and neglected. Some are victims of war or natural catastrophes, and no matter how much we try, we don't seem to have the resources to help most of them. In the days of Jesus, it was leprosy people feared; today it's cancer or AIDS. But Jesus still cares, and He expresses that care through us, His people. "Truly I tell you, whatever you did for one of the least of these brothers and sisters of mine, you did for me" (Matt. 25:40).

Our Inhumanity

The Lord is grieved by the way we mistreat His creation, but He is even more grieved by the way we mistreat each other, what Robert Burns called "man's inhumanity to man." After all, to abuse or destroy humanity is to attack the Lord, because we are made in the image of God (Gen. 9:5–6; James 3:9).

Did Mary ever tell her firstborn son that some

innocent boys in Bethlehem were killed because King Herod wanted to destroy Jesus?

When He went to Jerusalem at age twelve and stayed behind in the temple (Luke 2:41–50), did He detect the spiritual ignorance and hypocrisy of some of the religious leaders? Was He happy with what He saw in the temple? He returned home to Nazareth to eighteen years of obscurity as He learned carpentry and waited for the Father to tell Him what to do next. Did any of the customers try to cheat Joseph? Did some of them never pay for the work he did?

Certainly, as our Lord matured, He learned more and more about "man's inhumanity to man." At age thirty He began His public ministry and preached His first public message at the synagogue in Nazareth, His hometown— and they forced Him out of the building and tried to throw Him off a cliff (Luke 4:14–30)! The more popular Jesus became with the common people, the more the religious leaders envied Him and hated Him. Instead of listening carefully to His words and considering them, they said He was a liar and possessed of a demon. Instead of pondering His miracles, they said they were performed by Satan. Jesus reached the outcasts of society and transformed their lives, but instead of rejoicing, the religious leaders called Him "a glutton and a drunkard, a friend of tax collectors and sinners" (Luke 7:34). They set traps for Him so they could accuse Him of breaking God's law.

Most of the common people who followed Him weren't really sure who He was. They saw His miracles and listened to His messages, but were perplexed by the contradictory elements in His life. He claimed to have a kingdom, yet He labored like a common slave, serving the rich and the poor, men and women, Jews and Gentiles. He claimed to have no home of His own (Matt. 8:20), yet He was welcomed into the homes of a wide array of people. He claimed to forgive sins, yet both He and His disciples violated the traditions of the scribes and Pharisees. His own family didn't understand Him and said He was unbalanced (Mark 3:21, 31–35; Luke 8:19–21). Huge crowds of people followed Him, yet one day, an entire congregation got up and walked away, never to return (John 6:66–71). His own heart and mind were greatly pained by the unbelief and opposition of the religious leaders (Mark 3:1–6), and when He beheld the "holy city" of Jerusalem, He burst into tears and wept over their hardness of heart (Luke 19:41–44).

His Disciples

By the time our Lord was about to be arrested and crucified, He was pleased with the progress His disciples had made, Judas excluded. In the prayer recorded in John 17, Jesus was very complementary of them. They had accepted and obeyed the word Jesus gave them and knew that He had come from the Father (vv. 6–8). "And glory has come to me through them" (v. 10), a statement that reveals as much about Jesus the teacher as it does the disciples as learners. Jesus wanted the men to experience unity and joy in a world that hated them (vv. 13–14), and He asked the Father to protect them from the Evil One and set them apart by the truth of the Word (vv. 15–16). As soon as they received the empowerment of the Holy

Spirit, they would be able to go into the world with the message of Jesus Christ (v. 18).

These things encourage us, but they don't change the fact that there were times when the disciples were slow to understand spiritual truth. When Jesus descended the Mount of Transfiguration and found the nine disciples in a crowd around a demonized boy, He said, "You unbelieving and perverse generation, how long shall I stay with you? How long shall I put up with you?" (Matt. 17:17). The word "generation" included the boy's unbelieving father, the helpless disciples and the teachers of the law who were debating with them (Mark 9:14). Previously, Jesus had given the Twelve authority to cast out demons (Matt. 10:1–3, 8), but they must have failed in their personal walk and their faith, and the teachers of the law were making fun of their failure.

Yes, there were times when the men grieved the Master. They didn't understand His reference to yeast (Mark 8:14–21), and on at least two occasions, they tried to keep people from coming to Jesus for help (Matt. 15:21–28; 19:13–14). Unable to cast out a demon themselves, they tried to stop another man from casting out demons in the name of Jesus, and Jesus gently rebuked them (Mark 9:38–41). After His first mention of the cross, Jesus had to rebuke Peter for opposing Him, and then He taught the disciples what it meant to carry the cross (Matt. 16:21–18). When James and John asked permission to call down fire from heaven to punish an unfriendly Samaritan village, Jesus rebuked the brothers and led the Twelve to another village (Luke 9:51–56). Mary of Bethany anointed Jesus with expensive ointment, and

Judas criticized her and the other men joined him in the attack, But Jesus defended Mary and told them to leave her alone (Matt. 26:6–13; John 12:1–8).

In the upper room, as Jesus approached the "hour" the Father had appointed for His death (John 13:1), the disciples debated over which of them was the greatest (Luke 22:24–30). Jesus rebuked their proud competitive spirit by washing their feet (John 13:1–17).

Yes, the Twelve frequently misunderstood Jesus, disagreed with Him and disappointed Him, and in the Garden they abandoned Him; but Jesus knew that they would faithfully carry out His work after He returned to the Father and sent the Holy Spirit upon them.

His Father

Our Lord's three years of ministry were not easy, but He triumphed over obstacles and enemies *because of His relationship with His Father.* "The one who sent me is with me; he has not left me alone, for I always do what pleases him" (John 8:29). At His most difficult hour, when Judas would betray Him and His disciples would desert Him, He was able to say with confidence, "Yet I am not alone, for my Father is with me" (John 16:32). The Father, Son and Holy Spirit are with us today, so we need not fear (Heb. 13:5–6; Matt. 28:19–20; John 14:16).

Jesus was often encouraged by the Father in special ways. At our Lord's baptism, the Father spoke from heaven, "This is my Son, whom I love; with him I am well pleased" (Matt. 3:17), and the Spirit as a dove descended and rested on Jesus. The three Persons of the Godhead were united to "fulfill all righteousness" through the death, burial and resurrection of Jesus as symbolized in His baptism (Matt. 3:13–17; Luke 12:50). What a way to prepare for forty days of fasting and testing in the wilderness!

The Father spoke at the transfiguration when the Son experienced the glory He had laid aside when He came to earth (Matt. 17:1–8). What a way to get ready for the cross! Just before Jesus observed His last Passover, He was assured that His ministry had glorified the Father's name and that the Father's name would be glorified in Christ again (John 12:23–34). Our Lord's words in John 17:1 remind us of this scene. As Jesus prayed in the Garden, the three disciples closest to Him fell asleep, but the Father sent an angel to strengthen Him (Luke 22:43).

The Father prepared a body for Jesus so He could be born as a baby, experience human life and suffering, and eventually die as a sacrifice for sin (Heb. 10:1–10). His earthly life prepared Him to become our sympathetic high priest in heaven (Heb. 4:14–5:10). The Father gave Jesus "the Holy Spirit without limit" (John 3:34) so He could do the work assigned to Him. Each morning Jesus met with the Father and received His guidance for the day (Isa. 50:4–9).

During the humiliating suffering Jesus endured at the hands of sinners, He yielded Himself to the Father and trusted Him to see Him through. "When they hurled their insults at him, he did not retaliate; when he suffered, he made no threats. Instead he entrusted himself to him who judges justly" (1 Pet. 2:23). The tense of the verb translated "entrusted" indicates repeated action; the English Standard Version translates it "but continued entrusting himself . . . ." When Jesus died on the cross, the Father briefly forsook His Son (Ps. 22:1; Matt. 27:46) who was "made sin for us" (2 Cor. 5:21), yet at the same time the Father was "reconciling the world to himself in Christ" (2 Cor. 5:19)! Had that momentary forsaking not occurred, Jesus could not have cried "It is finished" (John 19:30), declaring that once and for all an adequate sacrifice had been made for the sins of the world (Heb. 10:1–18). The resurrection of Jesus Christ also involved the Father (Acts 2:22–24; Rom. 6:4), as did His ascension (Ps. 110; Acts 5:31; Phil. 2:9; 1 Pet. 1:21).

The Father's Encouragement

The Gospel of John records many of our Lord's statements concerning His relationship to the Father, and as you study them you can see how the Father gave the Son encouragement day after day. I suggest you read these texts and ponder each statement, because the Father encourages us today as He did His beloved Son.

The Father sent the Son (5:36–37, 43; 6:57; 8:16, 29; 12:49; 20:21). Knowing that we are where God wants us to be, doing what He wants us to do, is the foundation for a confident ministry, no matter how the Enemy may attack us. It was this kind of confidence that kept Jeremiah serving in spite of persecution and Nehemiah rebuilding the walls of Jerusalem in spite of the false accusations of his enemies and the discouragements of the work. When Jesus prayed to have the cup taken from Him, He added, "Yet not as I will, but as you will" (Matt. 26:39), and He taught us to pray that way as well: "your will be done, on earth as it is in heaven" (Matt. 6:10). If I know God has called me, equipped me and sent me, I can depend on Him to see me through.

The Father loves the Son (3:35; 5:20; 10:17; 14:31; 15:9–10; 17:24). Jesus wants His followers to experience God's love personally in their hearts and not just read about it in the Scriptures (14:21; 15:9–17; 17:23–26). The fact that the Father loves His people just as He loves His Son ought to thrill our hearts and help us love Him more. The will of God comes from the loving heart of God (Ps. 33:11), so we need never fear what He plans for us. "For Christ's love compels us," wrote Paul (2 Cor. 5:14).

The Father enabled His Son to minister (5:19, 36; 6:38; 17:4). The miracles Jesus performed were from the Father (5:14–19; 10:32, 37–38; 14:31), and so were the spiritual truths that He taught (8:28–29; 12:49–50; 14:24; 15:15; 17:8, 14). The scribes taught from authorities, but Jesus taught with authority, because His teachings came from God (Matt. 7:28–29). If we give ourselves to the study of His Word and obey it, the Lord will teach us and give us the words we need when we need them (Isaiah 50:4–5), and He will give us divine enablement to do the work He wants us to do (Phil. 4:13).

The Father answered His Son's prayers (11:41–42; 16:23–24; 15:16). Jesus rose early each morning to meet with His Father (Mark 1:35), and sometimes He spent all night in prayer (Luke 6:12). He prayed in the evening as well as in the morning (Mark 6:46) and fellowshipped with His Father during the entire day. He never allowed the crowd to keep Him from communing with the Father (Luke 5:15–16). We can come to the Father in the name of Jesus and He will hear us, love us and guide us.

The Father gives a people to His Son (6:40–45, 65; 10:27–30; 17:2, 6, 9, 24). Jesus ministered to great crowds, but not everybody who listened to Him or even experienced His healing power became a true disciple. While more than 500 people saw Him alive after His resurrection (1 Cor. 15:6), the church in Acts begins with 120 people (Acts 1:15). Jesus didn't accept everybody who said "Lord, Lord," because He knew the human heart (John 2:23–25). "All whom the Father gives me will come to me" (John 6:37). In His high priestly prayer (John 17), our Lord's favorite name for believers is "those you have given me" (17:2, 6, 9, 24). At the close of His earthly ministry, Jesus looked like a failure; but with the coming of the Spirit at Pentecost, God continued to call sinners to trust His Son just as He does today. Our ministry efforts would be useless if God did not "choose a people for his name" (Acts 15:14). "And the Lord added to their number daily those who were being saved" (Acts 2:47).

The Father mixed "the cup" and gave it to Jesus (John 18:11; see also Luke 22:39–44). In Scripture a cup symbolizes God's will and plan for a person (Ps. 16:5; Matt. 20:22–23). What happened to Jesus during Passover week in Jerusalem was not accidental or unexpected, for Jesus had already told His disciples what would happen. Peter told the Jewish crowd at Pentecost, "This man was handed over to you by God's deliberate plan and foreknowledge" (Acts 2:23) and a few days later, he told the crowd at the temple, "But this is how God fulfilled what he had foretold through all the prophets" (Acts 3:18). God will never mix a cup that will harm us, even though doing the will of God may occasionally bring pain. If we ask for a fish, our Father will never give us a snake (Luke 11:9–13).

The Father promised to transform suffering into glory and joy. Jesus prayed, "And now, Father, glorify me in your presence with the glory which I had with you before the world began" (John 17:5). First the suffering, then the glory (Luke 24:26). Our Lord had willingly laid aside His glory when He came to earth, and the Father promised to restore it when He returned to heaven. But this heavenly glory involves all of God's people. The key verses here are Hebrews 12:1–2: "And let us run with perseverance the race marked out for us, fixing our eyes on Jesus, the pioneer and perfecter of faith. For the joy set before him he endured the cross, scorning its shame, and sat down at the right hand of the throne of God."

What was "the joy set before him"? Perhaps Jude 24 gives us the answer: "To him who is able to keep you from stumbling and to present you before his glorious presence without fault and with great joy . . ." Jesus will present His glorified church before the Father, and as a part of the church ("those the Father gave to the Son"), we will share in both the glory and the joy. "Father, I want those you have given me to be with me where I am, and to see my glory." The cross and the cup will be replaced by the crown.

For some reason God's people today don't speak much about heaven, except at funeral services; but the glory and joy of heaven ought to be strong motivating forces in our lives no matter where we are. The assurance of heaven helped Jesus obey the Father's will in spite of shame, suffering, rejection and death; and it can do the same for us. As an old song puts it, "Who can mind the journey when the road leads home?"

His Joy

Our emphasis has been on suffering and glory, but perhaps I need to say something about the fact that Jesus also experienced joy. "At that time, Jesus, full of joy through the Holy Spirit, said, 'I praise you, Father, Lord of heaven and earth, because you have hidden these things from the wise and learned, and revealed them to little children. Yes, Father, for this was your good pleasure'" (Luke 10:21).

It gives the Father and the Son and the Holy Spirit great joy when God's people become as little children and humbly receive both the cup and the cross so that one day they might receive the joy and the crown. The trials we experience today are as nothing when compared to the joy that we will share when we see Jesus. We don't see Him with our physical eyes today, but we love Him just the same (1 Pet. 1:8), and knowing that we shall see Him in glory encourages us to keep on going, no matter how the Enemy may oppose us.

Never underestimate the present power of a future joy.

Abraham kept going because he saw a heavenly city. Jacob worked hard for an extra seven years because he saw a wedding and a bride whom he dearly loved. Jesus kept on going because He saw His bride, the church, in joyful glory on "Mount Zion . . . the city of the living God, the heavenly Jerusalem" (Heb. 12:22). Our citizenship is in that city (Phil. 3:20), and the wedding will be there!

For our light and momentary troubles are achieving for us an eternal glory that far outweighs them all. (2 Cor. 4:17)

Jesus resolutely set out for Jerusalem. (Luke 9:51)

Because the Sovereign LORD helps me, I will not be disgraced. Therefore I have set my face like flint. (Isa. 50:7)

It's always too soon to quit.

Endnotes

Introduction

1. Stuart Hamblen, "It Is No Secret What God Can Do" (song), 1950.

Chapter 3

1. Daniel J. Boorstin, *The Image: A Guide to Pseudo-Events in America* (New York: Harper Colophon Books, 1964), pp. 239–40. For twenty-five years Boorstin taught American History at the University of Chicago. He was also director of the Smithsonian Museum of American History and for twelve years the Librarian of Congress.
2. Brooks Atkinson, *Once Around the Sun* (New York: Harcourt, Brace and Company, 1951), p. 37.
3. Since Rachel, Joseph's mother, was dead, Jacob's mentioning of "your mother" in Genesis 37:10 probably refers to Leah who had stepped in to help raise Benjamin and Joseph. It's unlikely that the young Benjamin, Joseph's only full brother, joined the other ten in attacking Joseph.
4. Elie Wiesel, *Messengers of God* (NY: Simon and Schuster Touchstone Books, 1994), p. 166.

Chapter 4

1. James Boswell, *The Life of Samuel Johnson, Vol. III* (London: J.F. Dove, 1824), p. 257.
2. Christopher Morley, *Inward Ho!* (NY: Doubleday, Doran, 1931), p. 9.
3. J. Sidlow Baxter, *Awake My Heart!* (London: Marshall, Morgan and Scott, 1959), p. 216.

Chapter 5
1. God gave them their request, and they all died in the wilderness. See Numbers 14:20–35.
2. P.T. Forsyth, *Positive Preaching and the Modern Mind* (London: Independent Press, Ltd., 1953), p. 24.
3. Eric Hoffer, *Working and Thinking on the Waterfront* (NY: Harper & Row, 1969), p. 179.

Chapter 8
1. The prayers in the Book of Jeremiah are found in 1:6; 4:10; 9:1–3; 10:23–25; 12:1–4; 14:7–9; 14:19–22; 15:10, 15–18; 16:19–20; 17:12–18; 18:18–23; 20:7–18; 32:16–25 and chapter 42.

Chapter 10
1. If you have not read the Book of Nehemiah lately, I suggest you pause and do so before reading this chapter.
2. A Scottish word meaning "an old person who lives only in the past." It is probably related to the word "fog."
3. Charles H. Spurgeon, *Metropolitan Tabernacle Pulpit,* vol. 38, pp. 212–13.

Chapter 11
1. James McGinlay, *The Birthday of Souls* (Grand Rapids, MI: Wm. B. Eerdmans, 1941), pp. 29–48.

Chapter 12
1. Thomas Merton, *No Man Is an Island* (New York: Harcourt, Brace and Co., 1955).
2. Pronounced "prok-uh-pay," accent on the first syllable.

This book was produced by CLC Publications. We hope it has been life-changing and has given you a fresh experience of God through the work of the Holy Spirit. CLC Publications is an outreach of CLC Ministries International, a global literature mission with work in over 50 countries. If you would like to know more about us or are interested in opportunities to serve with a faith mission, we invite you to contact us at:

CLC Ministries International
P.O. Box 1449
Fort Washington, PA 19034

———

Phone: (215) 542-1242
E-mail: orders@clcpublications.com
Website: www.clcpublications.com

DO YOU LOVE GOOD CHRISTIAN BOOKS?
Do you have a heart for worldwide missions?

You can receive a FREE subscription to *CLC World*,
CLC's newsletter on global literature missions.

Order by e-mail at:
clcworld@clcusa.org

Or fill in the coupon below and mail to:
P.O. Box 1449
Fort Washington, PA 19034

FREE *CLC World* SUBSCRIPTION!

Name: _____

Address: _____

_____

Phone: _____ E-mail: _____

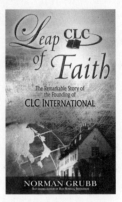